178
409
AK
24156
404
NAVY
B
168
NAVY
ATLANTA

JC
26997
E
USS INTREPID

MUSCLE PLANES

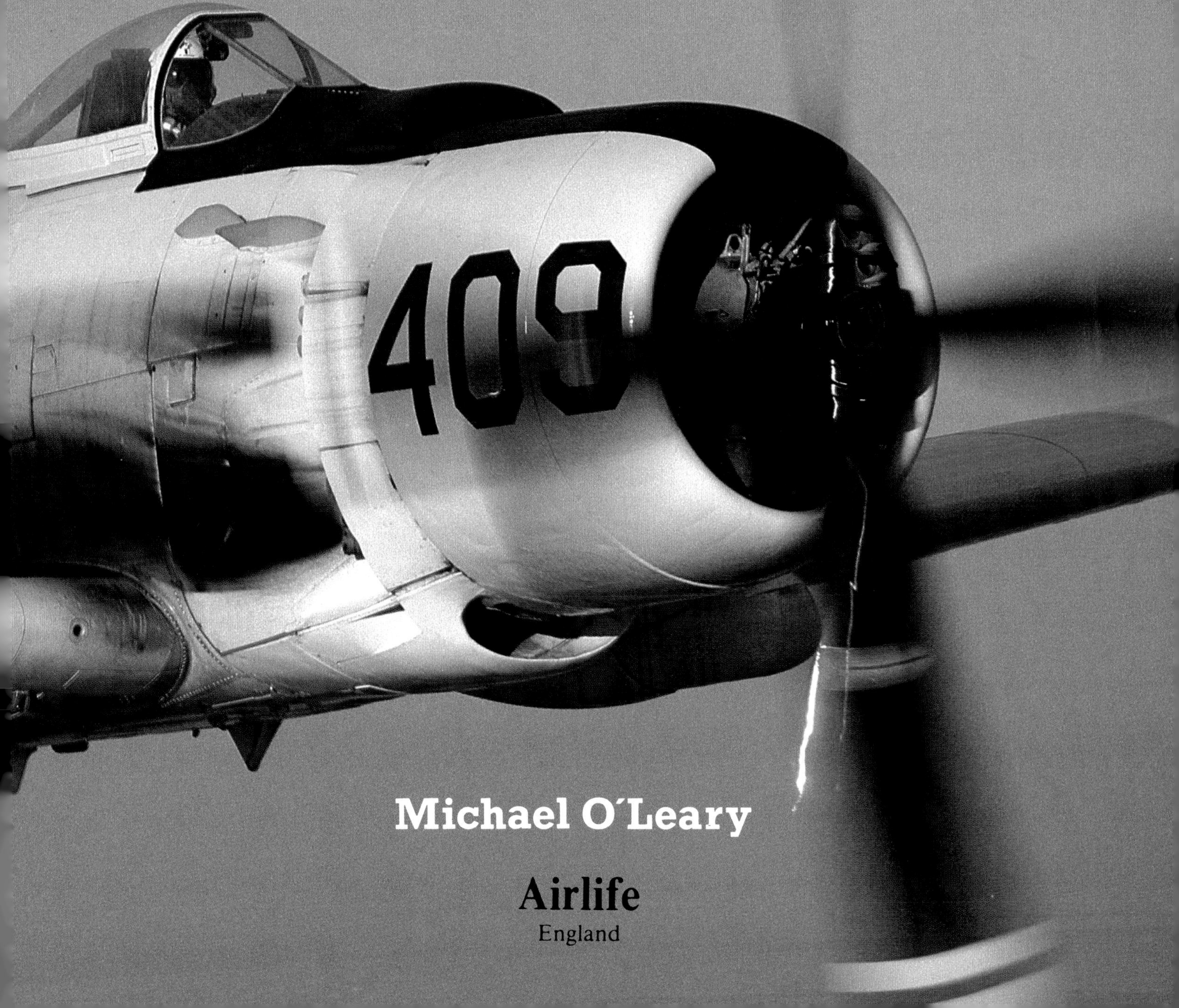

Michael O'Leary

Airlife
England

This edition first published in 1990 by Airlife Publishing Ltd., Shrewsbury, England

Published by Motorbooks International, P.O. Box 2, 729 Prospect Avenue, Osceola, WI 54020, USA, 1990

ISBN 1 85310 170 2

Printed and bound in Hong Kong

Airlife Publishing Ltd.
101 Longden Road, Shrewsbury, England

Acknowledgments

To create *Muscle Planes,* I called upon the support and help of many individuals, including Bruce Guberman, who was the camera plane pilot for many of the photographic sorties illustrated in this volume.

Brian Harrington, Paul Cronkwright, and Rick Franks of the Canadian Warplane Heritage made possible the chapter on the Hurricane. Ray and Mark Hanna, Howard Pardue and Stephen Grey contributed time and energy to recording the graceful lines of the Supermarine Spitfire.

Steve Stavrakakis and Ron Cox provided a useful insight to the world of airshow flying while doing the chapter on the diminutive biplane called the Green Machine.

Kermit Weeks, Linda Meyers, Vincent Tirado and the staff of the Weeks Air Museum were responsible for creating a most memorable day high above the Florida clouds with the museum's P-51D Mustang. In scenic Vancouver Island, Tom Irving and the staff of Forest Industries Flying Tankers made us welcome while we spent two glorious days with the mighty Martin Mars operated by the company.

The officers and men of the Montana and New Jersey Air National Guard provided an intimate look into the last operational days of the sleek Convair F-106 before the double-Mach interceptor was retired. Lieutenant John Hopkins and his staff aboard the USS *Theodore Roosevelt* went out of their way to show us the operational aspects of the mighty warship.

Once again, Howard Pardue and the members of the Breckenridge Air Museum along with members of the West Texas Wing of the Confederate Air Force provided sterling cooperation at the annual Breckenridge Air Show.

Foreword

When Motorbooks' publisher Tim Parker first approached me with the idea of a book on "muscle planes" I must admit that I was a bit puzzled. The confusion came through attempting to define the term. Followers of the horsepower-packed cars from the 60s and early 70s can easily define the term "muscle car." But what about muscle aircraft?

Muscle Planes is about aircraft that have the aura of power, about a definition of the magic of flight, about aircraft surrounded by a sense of wonderment with, perhaps, just a dash of danger thrown in for good measure.

Muscle Planes contains both civil and military aircraft, both ancient and modern planes, and aircraft with operational parameters ranging from civil transport, to professional air show aerobatics, to deadly military missions. *Muscle Planes* takes a look at aircraft that range in size from the miniscule sixteen-foot Green Machine to the monstrous Martin Mars, whose 200-foot wing span is still more than impressive—fifty years after the plane was built!

The aircraft featured on the following pages have the "right stuff" along with a definite glamour. And, yes, even the vintage Ford Tri-Motor, which was quite powerful for its day, is nostalgically glamorous as it rumbles overhead at a sedate 90 mph.

Michael O'Leary
Los Angeles, California

On the front cover: *Grumman engineers mated the powerful Pratt & Whitney R-2800 to a sleek, lightweight airframe to create the archetypical muscle plane—the Bearcat!*

On the back cover: *Kermit Weeks' P-51, one of the cleanest, most authentic Mustangs in the world.*

On the title page: *The tremendous power of the Skyraider's Wright R-3350 engine enabled it to carry an astonishing amount of weapons into battle.*

On the contents page: *Zooming straight up, the Convair F-106 Delta Dart is the vision of pure power.*

Contents

One more Tri: Ford Tri-Motor 6

First there was the Hurricane . . . 16

. . . And then there was the Spitfire 26

Green Machine: the Falcon Special 38

Every boy should have one: North American P-51 Mustang 46

Thunder from Port Alberni: Martin Mars 60

The last interceptor: Convair F-106 Delta Dart 72

The flying dump truck: Douglas Skyraider 82

Round-engine rodeo: Corsair and Wildcat, Avenger and Bearcat 92

US Navy's big stick: Carrier Attack Wing 110

One more Tri: Ford Tri-Motor

Titusville is one of many fading beach towns lining the Atlantic coast of Florida, perched just far enough away from the glitz of Disney World to not cash in on the profits but right next to Cape Canaveral's Space Shuttle flights. Titusville's airport, Dunn Airpark, is suffering too. A sign in the small office pleads, "Save the airport." Apparently the greed of the Florida developers is more than threatening the existence of the airport's rutted runway.

Parked in the weeds bordering the runway is a relic of a better time. The corrugated body of Ford Tri-Motor 4-AT-B-38 N7584 basks in the evening sun.

"Y'all ready to go?" asked lanky Ed Rusch, pilot and caretaker of this aeronautical anachronism. My friend Budd Davisson headed for the right seat of the Tri-Motor while I walked to the camera plane. The Tri-Motor's three radials burst to life and the plane rumbled gracefully into the air.

This Ford Tri-Motor (a wonderfully nostalgic term) was built in 1928. The veteran campaigner—one of the few sixty-year-old aircraft still flying, and one of even fewer still flying commercially—looks better today than when it was built. It originally sold for $54,000, and at that pre-Depression price it was a bargain, bringing the first really modern aerial transportation workhorse to purchaser Robertson Aircraft of Anglum, Missouri. Today, this vintage aircraft is worth well over $1,000,000.

N7584 was the first Tri-Motor to be purchased by Milt Hershberger, owner of Air Tours, Put-In-Bay, Ohio. When Hershberger founded Air Tours, he wanted something inexpensive that could haul passengers with a modicum of reliability. That plane was N7584, which he bought used for about three grand in 1935. He often had about a dozen Fords on hand, with three working the islands; N7584 was the first and the last.

N7584 first went into service with Air Tours in 1939. In 1947, Air Tours became known as Island Air Service, and the company operated a small fleet of vintage Fords. Island Air Service's primary business was the ferrying of school students to and from the Lake Erie islands; boat service was not then available. In this curious variant of school busing, young charges bound for educational advancement would board the Tri-Motors in the morning, returning to home and hearth in the evening.

Ed Rusch and N7584 share a common bond. Although the Ford is nearly twice Rusch's age, the two have crossed paths more than once. Rusch was a boat mechanic who got a pilot's license. He met some Island Airways people and when he found they needed another pilot, joined up—and then stayed for five years and 4,000 flying hours!

Rusch's last 600 hours at Island were in the classic Tri-Motor. "The longest stretch of water was only about a mile or so. You'd get right down on the deck and follow shore lines from airport to airport. It wasn't hard," said Rusch of his flying duties.

N7584's life came close to ending when, with another pilot aboard, a fuel blockage turned the Ford into a glider. The pilot tried to turn back to the field, but didn't make it. The Ford cartwheeled during the crash landing and was virtually demolished. But the crew and passengers escaped with only the slightest injuries, a testimonial to the rugged Ford airframe.

Island decided to have John Ellis and Kal-Aero in Kalamazoo, Michigan, rebuild the shattered airframe. It was an inevitable decision; to let the Ford die would have been a tragedy.

The Ford emerged from the rebuild in 1980 and was used just for special charters. It was then mothballed until it was sold to present owner Al Chaney in 1982. Chaney wanted to work the plane, to barnstorm and offer rides for a price. But he needed a pilot . . . enter Ed Rusch, again.

Since his Island days, Rusch had been flying Lears and MU-2s on night freight runs, and he was tired of the grind. Rusch wanted something different, and barnstorming the Ford across the United States, hopping rides for twenty dollars a seat, was certainly that. "It's the life of a gypsy," said Rusch. "You get to go to lots of different places and meet all sorts of people. It's fun. It's flying, and I really like it."

The Ford Tri-Motor is built like an aluminum bridge. It was made to be strong, since it was built before the day of computer stress analysis. It's a survivor, from the unusual construction to the wood steering wheels. The three Wright J-6 radials have fixed-pitch props and pump out 230 horses each. Starting is much like with an antique Ford truck. There's a starter solenoid for each engine between the rudder pedals. Rusch stomps on each solenoid and lets the prop go through a couple revolutions, and the engine bursts into life.

For a veteran with a load of passengers and fuel, the Ford performs well. It easily lifts off from short strips and claws aloft with surprising alacrity. This aircraft is a lesson in aeronautical honesty and efficiency. With a cruise speed of 95 mph and a landing speed of 55 mph, it requires considerable muscle input during flight, but handles rather like a large Piper Cub.

If the specter of liability insurance does not increase (it currently costs an astounding $70,000 a year to insure the Ford) and if the vintage airframe and engines keep holding together and functioning, there's a good chance that the Ford will be operating when it's a hundred years old.

N7584 is the last of the working Ford Tri-Motors, a bit of American aeronautical genius still earning its keep. Long may it fly!

Although a couple Tri-Motors are kept operational by wealthy antique aircraft collectors, N7584 is the only Tri-Motor still venturing forth to earn its daily keep by hauling passengers.

With a full load of paying passengers, the last working Ford Tri-Motor rumbles low over the Florida landscape. The Ford is slow—a factory brochure lists top speed at 114 mph, and that may be optimistic—and its low operating altitude offers a great chance for aeronautical sightseeing. Built in 1928, N7584 has survived many minor scrapes (along with one major accident) to keep on flying, and is today in even better shape than when originally rolled out of the Ford plant.

N7584
Ford
TRI-MOTOR
ISLAND AIRLINES

Henry Ford liked his mechanical contraptions to be simple and rugged; the Ford Tri-Motor does not lack in either category. This Ford is a working aircraft, and few customers are turned down. When a local skydiving club wanted to use the plane as a jump platform, Ed Rusch removed the passenger door and willingly obliged. The jumpers loved it!

Ford's distinctive logo identifies the aircraft to customers.

The Ford's wooden steering wheel also carries the company's logo. Henry Ford was a believer in advertising.

ISLAND AIRLINES
Ford
TRI-MOTOR

That big expanse of wing with its distinctive, utilitarian corrugated metal surface gets the Ford in and out of small strips with agility—something that was much appreciated by owners flying from the primitive airstrips of the twenties and thirties.

First there was the Hurricane . . .

Brian Harrington had pushed the throttles of the Twin Beech smartly forward, and we were moving along at a pretty good clip 2,000 feet above the rolling farmlands that surround Mt. Hope Airport in Hamilton, Ontario, Canada. We hàd removed the passenger door from the fuselage, and a fair wind was blasting around the entrance where Harrington had firmly secured me to the floor with a safety harness. Harrington, a member of the Canadian Warplane Heritage (CWH), sponsors and flies the vintage Twin Beech and is responsible for the beautifully maintained transport's health and care. On this clear and crisp June morning, the Beech had lost its vintage transport role, becoming a camera platform.

The object of our mission quickly appeared. Rick Franks roared under the Beech in the Hawker Hurricane, gained a fistful of altitude, stood the fighter on its right wing and then shot out of sight beneath us. The Hurricane was the sole purpose of our mission.

The ultra-rare early World War II fighter was acquired by the CWH after protracted negotiations and became one of the most important displays of the living museum, almost all of whose vintage aircraft are maintained in magnificent flying condition so they can be displayed where they belong—in the air!

The Hawker Hurricane was the first "modern" fighter for the Royal Air Force (RAF), a distinction it owes almost to chance rather than careful planning. Following the Great War, the RAF relied on a series of limited production biplane fighters for the defense of the United Kingdom. Postwar defense budgets were minimal to say the least, and the new generation of biplane fighters did not have much to offer over their World War One counterparts. In 1933, the defense of Britain relied on just thirteen fighter squadrons—eight equipped with Bristol Bulldogs (maximum speed 174 mph), two with Hawker Demons (maximum speed 182 mph) and three with Hawker Furys (maximum speed 204 mph). There were few fighter aircraft more sublime than the art deco-stylized Fury. However, the Fury was more of a rich man's high-performance sporting plane than a real interceptor. Not all that far away, in Germany, a madman and his collection of toadies were formulating a plan that would make aircraft like those the RAF operated worse than obsolete.

During this time period, work started on the Messerschmitt Bf 109—a design that would burn its name in history. High-placed British officials knew the Germans had exceeded the limits of the Disarmament Conference and were proceeding on a rapid, if clandestine, build-up of military arms, including their air force, or Luftwaffe.

In Britain, certain designers were still pushing the biplane as the ultimate aerial fighter. It's true that the plane's two wings offered sterling maneuverability, but its built-in drag, fixed landing gear, limited performance and range meant that the biplane was no longer the choice of designers concerned with the ever-changing global situation.

Sydney Camm of Hawker had come up with a couple monoplane designs and was trying to point the company toward the future. One of these designs, using the Fury as its basis, quickly found favor. The new design, coming out among warnings from Churchill about a new, militant Germany, used the basic (and rather primitive) structure of the Fury mated to a thick monoplane wing with retractable landing gear, enclosed cockpit and a Goshawk engine giving a projected speed of about 260 mph.

By today's standards, everything about the new design was fairly crude, even the landing gear, which the British apparently had a problem making retractable. A number of different armament combinations were considered, but the final choice was the Colt Automatic Weapon Corporation .30 caliber machine gun modified to take the British .303 cartridge. The Ministry of Defense then issued draft Specification F.5/34 (F for fighter, 5 for the fifth fighter design and 34 for 1934) for a fighter that would have an armament of eight to ten of these weapons. Hawker went ahead with a private venture project that would satisfy the Air Ministry specification. A final design (F.36/34 Single-Seat Fighter—High Speed Monoplane) was sent to the government on 4 September 1934, and construction started in the Hawker shops.

As study of the design progressed, the Goshawk engine was replaced with the Rolls-Royce PV-12, which provided about forty percent more power with little increased frontal area or weight penalty. Much faith was placed on this new engine, which offered unheard-of reliability and available power. Its slim frontal area made streamlining much easier, while the basic design also showed a great deal of growth potential. The name Merlin was allocated to the PV-12, and history was in the making.

Construction proceeded at a quick rate—unlike today, when design-to-production times can run into years—and the prototype made its first flight on 6 November 1935, from Brooklands (which also doubled as a motor racing course) with company test pilot P.W.S. George Bulman at the controls. Doped silver overall and carrying Royal Air Force serial number K5083, the first Hawker Hurricane was an attractive aircraft.

Testing moved forward as fast as possible, with airframe and engine bugs slowing down the schedule a bit; the second flight was on November

11, the third on November 23 and the fourth on November 26. As with any new aircraft, many minor modifications were undertaken as flight testing continued. The canopy was strengthened, tailplane struts removed and a radio installed. Performance indicated a top speed of 315 mph at 16,200 feet—a vast improvement over the earlier biplanes.

The British government realized that the situation in Europe was extremely dangerous and that the underequipped RAF needed new high-performance fighters. Accordingly, on 3 June 1936, a contract was placed with Hawker Aircraft for the production of 600 aircraft with the officially approved name of Hurricane. The size of the order stunned British industry; it was the largest peacetime order ever placed, and it did not reflect the fact that Hawker Aircraft still had to produce about 500 Hart biplane variants over the next couple of years.

Suddenly the Hawker factory was swamped with work, and much hiring and expansion had to be rapidly undertaken while a new production factory was built at Parlunt Park Farm, Langley, for the sole purpose of building Hurricanes. This factory alone went on to build over 7,000 of the sturdy fighters.

While all this was going on, the prototype was being flown and continually modified to create an aircraft that would be close to production standards. Much testing was taken with the new Merlins, some of which were having a hard time surviving past the fifty-flight-hours

continued on page 18

The first Hurricanes were equipped with a fixed-pitch, two-blade wooden propeller. Later models were fitted with three-blade controllable-pitch units that greatly increased performance.

continued from page 17
mark. The Merlin II was standardized for production, and one of these engines was mated to the first production machine, L1547, which flew for the first time on 12 October 1937, with Philip Lucas in the cockpit. Painted a drab camouflage, an ominous sign of the hard times to come, this aircraft carried eight Browning machine guns. By the next month, L1547 had been joined by six more aircraft for flight testing and squadron acceptance trials. The high volume of aircraft pouring from the Hawker factories meant that the four company test pilots undertook 3,200 test flights during 1938 alone!

The first squadron to receive the new fighter was No. 111 Squadron at RAF Northolt in the northern sector of London. The squadron had one flight of Hurricane Mk. Is on the line by December 1937 and was fully equipped by January 1938—giving some idea of the urgency of the situation and just how quickly fighter aircraft could be produced back then.

Other squadrons (including Nos. 3 and 56) also came up to strength quickly, and accidents were soon taking place as pilots tried to get familiar with their new and complex aircraft. Accidents that were not particularly destructive were usually easily repaired, owing to the Hurricane's simple and robust construction. The entire aircraft, except for metal panels, was fabric-covered—mainly because Hawker did not have sufficient state-of-the-art knowledge to produce metal-covered airframes when the Hurricane went into production!

Various improvements were instigated on the Hurricane production line as more and more aircraft flowed from the factory. One of these was the
continued on page 20

The early World War II camouflage of the Hurricane Mk. IIB blends neatly with the rural countryside.

continued from page 18
fitting of metal-covered wings, which began in April 1939. At the same time, emphasis was put on providing the Hurricane with a modicum of armor protection for the systems and pilot. The first of the fighters to appear with pilot armor protection was delivered in February 1940. Armament upgrades were also considered, and some Hurricanes were tested with 20 mm cannon, one hung under each wing panel.

Since the demand for the fighter was so great, production was licensed to Gloster Aircraft, which delivered its first aircraft in October 1939 and delivered a thousand Hurricanes by the end of 1940. Production of the Hurricane Mk. I totaled 1,924 aircraft by Hawker and 1,850 by Gloster.

Production of the Hurricane was also licensed to the Canadian Car and Foundry Company in Canada. In November 1938, that company received a contract for the production of forty Hurricanes. The British shipped a pattern aircraft to Canada along with all the necessary blueprints and drawings, and the complex process of creating a duplicate fighter began. The first Canadian Hurricane was delivered on 9 January 1940, with production going on to encompass 1,450 machines.

At the start of World War Two, the RAF had eighteen fighter squadrons equipped with the Hurricane. Two of the units (Nos. 1

and 73 Squadrons) were sent to France as part of the British Expeditionary Force. These units were soon reinforced by several more squadrons, all of which sat around rather smugly during the strange interlude known as the Phoney War.

When the Germans started to move in May 1940, six more Hurricane squadrons were quickly dispatched to the Continent. The Hurricanes enjoyed some success against the advancing Germans, but victory was on the side of the enemy. The swiftly advancing blitzkrieg soon accounted for about one-fourth of the RAF's operational fighter strength—with aircraft either destroyed in combat or simply abandoned by Brits anxious to escape from bases that were rapidly overrun by the enemy.

Quick production of the Hurricane meant that over 2,300 aircraft were delivered by August 1940, equipping thirty-two squadrons

continued on page 24

Rick Franks banks the Hurricane for the camera plane. Fitted with a twelve-gun wing containing Browning .303 weapons, the fighter was a quantum leap from previous biplanes that usually carried just a pair of the weapons. A big, bulky aircraft that has little of the innate grace of the Spitfire, the Hurricane was the fighter that stopped the Germans during the Battle of Britain.

The Merlin engine provided the rugged Hurricane with lots of power and went on to be one of the greatest combat power-plants ever built. The three stub ejector stacks were found to increase airspeed by two mph.

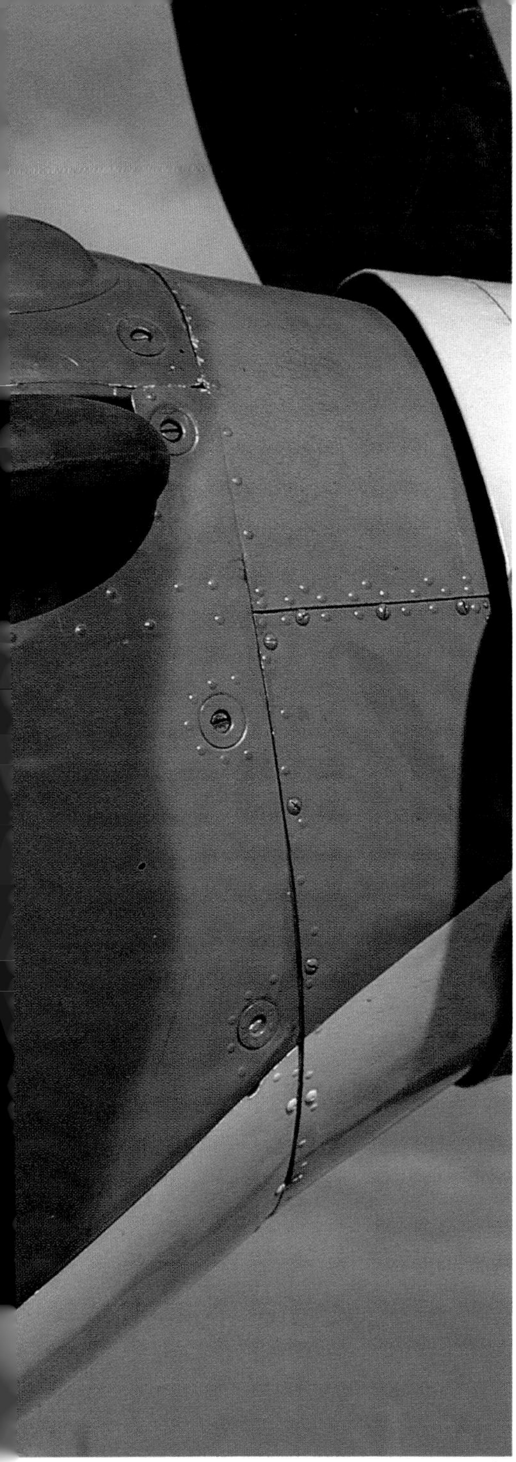

The small cockpit is entered through a folding hatch on the right side of the fuselage. The red paint covered fabric patches that were put over the gun ports to protect the weapons from dirt until they were fired.

continued from page 21
while nineteen squadrons flew the more elegant Spitfire. When the Battle of Britain began, it was the Hurricane that rose in considerable numbers to encounter the marauding Luftwaffe. Even though somewhat inferior to the enemy aircraft, the Hurricane did its job—especially taking on and defeating the enemy's bomber force while the Spitfires tackled the supporting fighters.

While the Battle of Britain raged, a number of modifications were considered to improve the Hurricane's combat potential. Uprated engines were installed. With the installation of the Merlin XX (offering 1280 hp at takeoff) the Hurricane Mk. II was born. Two sets of wings were designed for the new variant, including one with twelve .303 caliber weapons and another with four 20 mm Oerlikon cannon.

The new wings could also accommodate bombs and rockets, and the Hurricane began a new career in ground attack as more improved Spitfires took over the fighter role. Hurricanes began deployment in all theaters of war, some being modified for seagoing service as Sea Hurricanes or, even stranger, as Hurricats—fighters to be catapulted off merchant ships to counter the threat of enemy FW 200 Kondor bombers, with the only choice after launching being a crash-landing in the ocean.

Even though quickly outmoded by advancing combat aircraft designs, the Hurricane equipped the RAF around the world, fighting on every front. Battling with the British and their allies, the Hawker fighter continued to be praised for its ruggedness and reliability. Nevertheless, when large quantities of new fighters became available, production of the Hurricane ceased in September 1944. Total production amounted to 14,233 aircraft, including 1,451 fighters built under license in Canada.

Royal Canadian Air Force (RCAF) 5377 is a Canadian-built Hurricane that is still flying—a rarity. Most surviving Hurricanes were quickly scrapped at the war's end, and of the dozen or so remaining examples only a few are still airworthy.

The Hurricanes were the first modern fighter aircraft built in Canada, and the Canadian version differed a bit from the British aircraft. All Canadian-built machines had wings covered with aluminum alloy rather than fabric, and many of the Canadian machines had Packard-built Merlins rather than Rolls-Royce units.

Problems with getting some British-built supplies arose during the darkest days of the war, and many Hurricanes were fitted with cut-down Fairey Battle propellers. Other problems arose with some Packard engines, which had to be returned to the factory for modification.

As Hurricanes began to pour from the Canadian Car and Foundry production line, the fighters were sent to all parts of the globe where the empire was fighting for survival, with some machines reserved for the defense of the Canadian west coast. RCAF 5377 first went into service with the RCAF during late 1942 when it joined No. 133 Squadron. The fighter was used for coastal defense duties and in a training role during the war. At the end of hostilities, the plane was sold surplus in Manitoba.

Sold from huge lots, many Hurricanes were snapped up by local farmers who dragged their new prizes (with the wings off) home, where the airframes were picked apart for years to provide useful bits and pieces for life and work around the farm. Subjected to such scavenging combined with the harsh Canadian winters, the once-proud Hurricane fleet slowly began to return to nature.

In the late sixties, a movement to preserve and fly historic World War Two aircraft began and collector Bob Diemert gathered derelict aircraft from the farms surrounding his Carmen, Manitoba, base. Most of the machines were incomplete, but one was not as bad as the others; this was Hurricane Mk. IIB construction number 42012, RCAF 5377. Diemert decided to begin a rebuild and went to work. At that time only one Hurricane in Britain was still flying; Diemert's restoration doubled the flying population.

In 1968, producers gathered vintage aircraft for the film *Battle of Britain*. Diemert's Hurricane was purchased and transported to Britain, where it appeared in the epic movie.

The plane was eventually purchased by Sir William Roberts, Strathallan, Scotland. Roberts wanted the historic fighter for his growing vintage aircraft collection. When the fighter arrived in Scotland, Roberts was put off by the quality of the original restoration, so he set his team to work on a lengthy rebuild that would return the fighter to as stock a condition as possible. The Scottish rebuild took several years to complete, but when finished the Hurricane was in pristine condition.

The plane rarely flew. Several years ago, Roberts decided to auction the Hurricane along with some of his other aircraft in order to consolidate his collection. The Hurricane was purchased by the Roberts family trust so that it would be kept in Britain.

The fighter was offered for sale again in 1984. Dennis Bradley, founder of the Canadian Warplane Heritage, felt the aircraft was of such historic importance that every effort should be undertaken to return the Hurricane to Canada.

The purchase—at a price far removed from the plane's original $50 surplus sale price—became possible through the generous assistance of the Molson Companies and the Molson Family Foundation, and through contributions from former members of No. 1/401 Squadron RCAF and friends of the CWH. The Canadian government recognized the outstanding historic significance of the Hurricane through a major grant from the Cultural Property Department of the Ministry of Communications. And the No. 436 Squadron of the

The CWH Hurricane appears here in formation with two other classic CWH fighters: a P-51D Mustang flown by Dennis Bradley and an FG-1D Corsair flown by Peter Gutowski. Not long after this photo was taken, the Mustang was destroyed in a forced landing following engine failure. Both occupants escaped injury.

Canadian Armed Forces from Trenton transported the Hurricane from Scotland to the CWH museum in Hamilton using one of its C-130 Hercules transports.

The Hurricane was erected and given a thorough inspection before a test flight, and several hours were accumulated by the time of the CWH's tenth anniversary air show, in 1984. There is little doubt that the Hurricane was the star of that show.

RCAF 5377 (previously registered CF-SMI and G-AWLW, now registered C-GCWH) is the only flying Hurricane in North America. Happily, however, its status is being challenged as several other rebuilds are now nearing completion.

. . . And then there was the Spitfire

Muscle planes come in all sizes and shapes, but the muscle plane with the most finesse is the Supermarine Spitfire. This aircraft's fine lines and elegant elliptical wing combine to give the impression of an artistic statement rather than that of a mechanical warrior.

The Spitfire revolutionized Britain's fighter forces, but the aircraft was also part of a worldwide revolution in combat plane designs; equally deadly and efficient combat aircraft were created in several parts of the world, notably Germany. The Spitfire design did not break new ground in aviation design, but the aircraft did meld modern components of combat aviation into a fighter that was a success from the first moment it flew.

The Spitfire was given birth by the creative mind of R. J. Mitchell, chief designer of the small firm of Supermarine—a company whose main occupation had been building a variety of seaplanes. Mitchell designed the Spitfire in 1935, and the first prototype took to the air a year later. Over 22,000 Spitfires of forty-eight different Marks were produced in a manufacturing life of over eleven years, a wonderful achievement when one considers that the average combat aircraft of that era usually had a production run of just a few years.

As much as the success of the Spitfire depended on the genius of R.J. Mitchell, the fighter also depended very heavily on the Rolls-Royce Merlin that powered it. Developed from the engine used in the Schneider Trophy racers, the Merlin was the right powerplant at the right time. Seldom in the history of fighter aircraft design has such a perfect combination of airframe and engine been achieved.

Test pilot Mutt Summers took the prototype Spitfire aloft for its first flight on 5 March 1936. Upon landing, he commented, "Don't touch anything."

Little did Summers realize just how much the Spitfire would change over its operational life. Tests on the prototype led directly to production of the Spitfire Mk. I, which differed only in a number of minor ways. Production of the Spitfire was much more complex than production of the Hawker Hurricane, however—especially since the government required that three-quarters of Spitfire production be subcontracted, leading to comments regarding England's cottage industry method of production.

The graceful wing of the Spitfire neatly housed eight .303 caliber Browning air-cooled machine guns and was a strong point of the Mitchell design. The use of a thin airfoil meant that a higher speed could be attained, but a thin section also meant that fitting of military equipment (such as guns) would require precise engineering. The elliptical wing proved to have an added benefit when it was discovered that it had lower induced drag, thus allowing for more efficient operation at high altitude. This was particularly advantageous for photo reconnaissance variants.

Mitchell saw the first flights of the prototype but he was in poor health due to cancer and, shortly afterward, passed away without seeing his design in combat over the skies of Britain. As production of the Mk. I, with its fixed-pitch two-blade wooden propeller, built up, No. 19 Squadron at Duxford became the first unit to receive operational fighters, the first example being delivered on 29 July 1938.

When Britain entered the war on 3 September 1939, nine squadrons of operational Spitfires stood at the ready, and more Spitfires poured from the production lines as mass production problems were gradually overcome. The government, wisely, decided to send Hurricane units to France and reserve the Spitfire squadrons on home soil. There was a bit of practicality in this thinking, since the Hurricane's structure was more robust and suited for operations out of the rather primitive French airfields.

Modifications came fast and furious as the Spits flowed from the factories. New and more powerful Merlins were quickly added, along with much more efficient three-blade constant-speed propellers. Among numerous other changes were several to the wings.

It appears that early in the design of the Spitfire, Mitchell considered installing cannon armament in the wing, but this idea was not taken up. Early in the war, however, it was found that the combined punch of the eight rifle-caliber Brownings was often not enough to bring down a German bomber. Wings were experimentally fitted to house Browning 20 mm cannon, and this concept was found to be successful although a number of early installation problems followed. This modification led to three distinct types of Spitfire wings, each distinguished with a letter of the alphabet following the Mark's designation: A meant an armament of eight .303s was carried; B indicated two 20 mm British Hispano cannon plus four .303 machine guns; and C, the so-called universal wing, was equipped to house a variety of machine gun and cannon installations. Thus, a Spitfire Mk. IXB variant mounted the cannon and Brownings.

Performance was paramount as the war progressed, and new variants constantly appeared to combat new Luftwaffe threats. The Mk. V was built to perform at high altitudes and was fitted with the more powerful Merlin 45, which had a more effective supercharger giving 1315 hp at

16,000 feet, providing a marked edge in performance over the Messerschmitt Bf 109F, which first flew in combat in May 1941.

The Mk. IX was basically a Mark V equipped with a Merlin 61 and was ordered into production to counter the unexpected arrival of the Focke-Wulk Fw 190A. The new engine enabled much higher power settings to be employed during battle. Tests with a captured 190 showed that the Mk. IX stood a good chance of victory if the pilot was able to gain the initial advantage. The Fw 190 had a superior rate of roll, was faster in a dive and was more maneuverable overall, but the Mk. IX could outturn it. At most altitudes, the Spitfire also had a slight speed advantage, but even so, the Fw 190 was a difficult and deadly opponent.

This type of development continued throughout the war as the British tried to stay ahead of the

continued on page 30

Howard Pardue has made the Spitfire a fairly common sight in the skies over Texas. Pardue sponsors the Confederate Air Force's Mk. IXC and keeps the fighter in fine flying trim at his Breckenridge home base.

Throughout its production life, the Spitfire was constantly changing. The small canopy on the Mk. IX eventually gave way to a bubble unit on later variants.

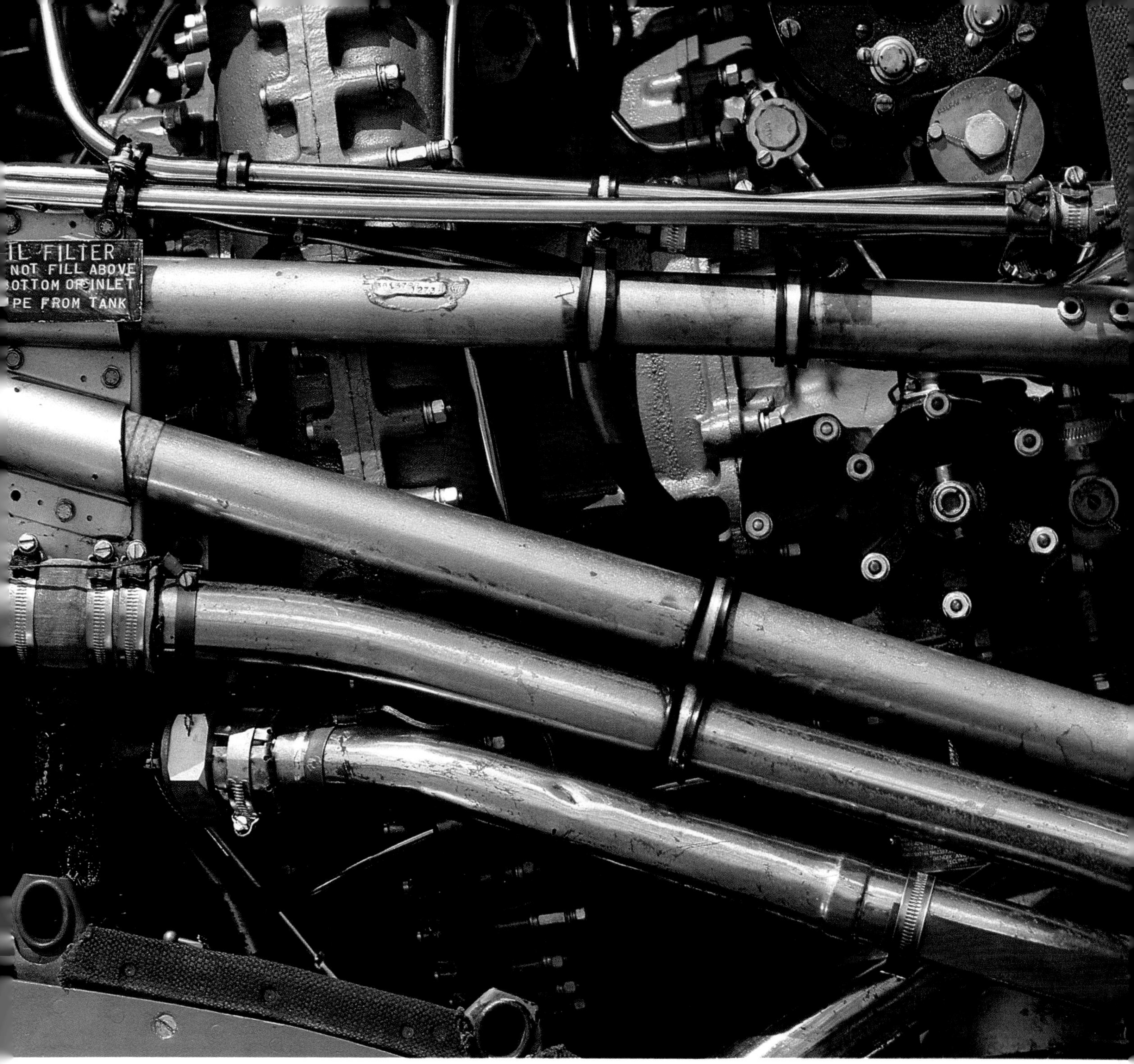

A mass of beautifully detailed plumbing highlights the Merlin powerplant in Stephen Grey's Spitfire Mk. IXE ML417. Probably one of the most efficient combat engines ever produced, the Rolls-Royce Merlin (built in a modified form in the United States by Packard) is now an engine much in demand for restored Spitfires and Mustangs, and supplies of parts are running thin.

continued from page 27
Germans. Later variants of the Spitfire were equipped with the mighty Rolls-Royce Griffon, and a redesign of the airframe was required to adapt the plane to the increased horsepower available from this excellent V-12 powerplant. With the Mk. XX, the Spitfire's wing plan was drastically altered to give extra strength, accept greater airframe weights and allow better performance at higher altitudes. (Also with the Mk. 21, the Spitfire Mark series designations switched from roman numerals to arabic numbers.)

Just to go through all the Mark changes and combat exploits of the Spitfire would fill many volumes (and has!), but here are a few salient facts: from the Mk. I to the Mk. 21, the top speed of the Spitfire increased by 100 mph; gross weight increased from 5,800 lb. to over 11,000 lb.; engine horsepower went from 1020 to 2100; and the airframe was adapted for a wide variety of missions, including interceptor, ground attack, high-altitude photo reconnaissance, bomber escort and air-sea rescue.

About twenty-four Spitfires remain airworthy, but such is the interest (and value) of this classic warplane that an almost equal number are currently under restoration to flying status, and an active search continues around the globe for airframes, parts and engines that can be made flyable.

One of these Spitfires, Mk. IX MH434 carrying British civil registration G-ASJV, is owned by famed British air show pilot Ray Hanna. The plane is usually present at the biggest European and British air
continued on page 31

With the wooden-bladed Rotol propeller, the engine would suffer little, if any, damage if the aircraft tipped on its nose while taxiing. The wooden blades would splinter, whereas metal blades would simply shock-load the engine—probably destroying the powerplant.

continued from page 30
displays flown by Hanna or his son Mark who was an RAF Phantom pilot.

MH434 is a historic airframe. Built at the Spitfire factory in Castle Bromwich, this Mk. IX was assigned to No. 222 "Natal" Squadron at Hornchurch on 17 August 1943. While with No. 222, MH434 was flown by Flight Lieutenant H. P. Lardner Burke, who shot down an Fw 190 on 27 August 1943, while escorting a flight of American B-17 Flying Fortresses. During this fight, Burke also damaged another Fw 190. Burke scored further success on the 5th of September when he knocked down another Fw 190, and on the 8th when he shared a Bf 109 kill with another pilot.

At this point, MH434 was transferred to No. 350 Squadron, but it returned to No. 222 in March 1944. An accident on 7 July 1944, put the fighter out of commission for the rest of the year. Repair was not completed until 19 April 1945, after which there was no operational need for the Spit.

The aircraft was moved through several maintenance units until being struck off charge on 19 April 1946—at which time it was stored until being sold to the Dutch government on 19 February 1947. It was then carefully disassembled and shipped by boat to the Dutch East Indies, arriving on 22 July 1947.

Given the code H-105, the fighter was assigned to No. 322 Squadron at Semarang on 22 December 1947. It was renumbered H-68 in 1948 and flew many counterinsurgency missions against
continued on page 32

A small door folds on the left side of the Spitfire's fuselage, making entry or exit through the small opening created by the sliding canopy much easier. A small crowbar was attached to the inside of the entry door to aid the pilot in the event of a crash landing. Sometimes the sliding hood would jam, and the pilot would need the crowbar to escape from the aircraft.

continued from page 31
rebels, but was belly-landed following hydraulic failure on 7 May 1949.

Shipped back to Rotterdam, the fighter was overhauled and repaired by Fokker, flying again on 10 March 1953. Next the Spitfire was sold to the Belgian Air Force as SM-41, where it was used at a training school and then assigned to No. 13 Wing.

MH434 was sold surplus in 1956, was given the Belgium civil registration OO-ARA and was operated by COGEA Nouvelle at Ostende starting on 23 March of the same year. Used in an antiaircraft cooperation role, the fighter was eventually sold to British pilot Tim Davies on 3 July 1963 and was flown to Britain for an overhaul and a repaint in a beautiful blue, silver and white scheme.

Sold once again on 23 November 1967, the Spit became a star in the epic film *Battle of Britain.* After that it was purchased by Adrian Swire on 23 February 1969. He used the aircraft for pleasure flights. During Swire's ownership, MH434 appeared in the film *A Bridge Too Far.*

After being sold to Ray Hanna, the Spitfire was beautifully finished in its wartime markings. While in Hannas's ownership, the Spitfire has appeared in many air shows and in several films and television programs. It is one of a number of vintage warplanes in Hanna's Old Flying Machine Company, and is based at the historic Imperial War Museum airfield of Duxford (where the first operational Spitfire squadron served).

Another surviving Mk. IX calls Breckenridge, Texas, home. The sprawling Texas midlands are an odd place to find a Spit—but Texan Howard Pardue is the chief sponsor

continued on page 34

Registered NX9BL, the CAF Spitfire carries the markings of RAF ace Douglas Bader. With power pulled back, Pardue circles over downtown Breckenridge. Note the open radiator shutters.

D
B
MK297

continued from page 32
for the aircraft, which is owned by the Confederate Air Force, and Pardue maintains and flies the fighter from his home field.

This plane, which was built with Royal Air Force serial number MK297, has a history as long and complex as that of Ray Hanna's aircraft. After serving with the RAF, it went to the Royal Netherlands Air Force, where it operated with serial numbers H-55 and H-116. It then went to the Belgian Air Force as SM-43. After being surplused, it was purchased by COGEA and used as a target tug with the registration OO-ARB. It was sold to a private owner in Britain during the mid-sixties as G-ASSD.

The CAF obtained the Mk. IX in the late sixties after the conclusion of filming for *Battle of Britain,* and the plane became N1882. It was flown for several years at CAF air shows, then was finally grounded and completely rebuilt. The Spit emerged from the restoration shop in fine condition and was registered NX9BL. It flew until being heavily damaged in a forced landing after running out of fuel. After being rebuilt once again, it flew only occasionally.

In the early eighties, sponsorship for the Mk. IX was taken over by CAF members Howard Pardue and Jack Gaulding (before Gaulding's death in a 1987 T-28 crash). Pardue and Gaulding saw that the Spitfire needed lots of work to get it back into reasonable flying shape. The plane was transferred to Pardue's Breckenridge base where a new fuel tank was installed, extra fuel tanks were placed in the wings (adding fifty gallons), a new windshield was installed, sheet metal repairs were done, a new engine aftercooler was installed and many other minor repairs were completed.

The Spit is now in fine condition, and the additional fuel gives a range that makes it practical to take the fighter to air shows around the United States. In 1988, Pardue flew the fighter for the British television miniseries *Piece of Cake.* A film unit traveled to Texas to shoot the Spitfire attacking the CAF's Heinkel He-111 (the only flying example in the world).

Stephen Grey is a pillar of Britain's rapidly growing Warbird movement. Grey headquarters his constantly expanding fleet (ranging from a rare Bell P-63 Kingcobra to a North American B-25D Mitchell) at the Imperial War Museum airfield of Duxford, near the British university town of Cambridge. Known as the Fighter Collection, these fabulous World War II fighting machines (the Mitchell bomber is used as a crew transport) are all either in flying condition or being restored to flying condition.

One star of the collection is Spitfire Mk. IXE ML417, which is maintained in immaculate condition and is one of Grey's favorite aircraft. This plane was delivered to the RAF in April 1944 and allocated to No. 443 Royal Canadian Air Force Squadron at Ford in Sussex. When with that unit, the plane was given the individual code letters 2I-T.

This Spitfire had a long and significant combat history. The No. 443 Squadron was heavily involved in the invasion of France. On 26 June 1944, a Fw 190 was damaged by ML417 in a dogfight over Rouen while the Spit was flown by Flight Lieutenant W. A. Prest. On 9 July, ML417 made an emergency landing at St. Croix after being damaged by flak, and repairs were undertaken before the fighter returned to its unit.

ML417 was quickly back in action. On 13 July 1944, a Bf 109 was damaged by Flt. Lt. Prest in action over Normandy. Meeting heavy German resistance, ML417 was again damaged by flak on 25 July and 7 August, but repairs were carried out after each incident.

In action near La Culot, Belgium, on 29 September 1944, two Bf 109s were claimed destroyed while ML417 was flown by Flying Officer R. A. Hodgins. The Spitfire received damage during this action, and was subsequently repaired. The fighter returned to its squadron in October.

In October 1944, the fighter was transferred to No. 442 Squadron and then to No. 401 Squadron. It returned to No. 443 in March 1945, then went to No. 441 on 5 April, back to No. 442, off to No. 412 Squadron and then to No. 411 Squadron on 29 June. All of these were RCAF squadrons; these moves show how aircraft were transferred as combat needs dictated.

At the end of the war in Europe, thousands of Spitfires were put into storage pending disposal or scrapping. ML417 was one of the aircraft consigned to huge storage lots. In October 1946, it was purchased by Vickers Armstrong for conversion to a two-seat dual-control trainer. (It's odd that an aircraft with a history of fairly extensive battle damage was picked for conversion, especially since such a vast choice of airframes was available.)

By 1948, the ungainly modification was carried out. The rebuilt Spitfire featured a large bubble canopy on the fuselage spine, housing the instructor and the instructor's set of controls, and the original cockpit had been moved forward one foot to accommodate the student. The plane was sold to the Indian Air Force.

After World War II, the Indian Air Force operated Spitfires extensively. When their service lives were over, the machines were either scrapped or placed on airfield boundaries where they were used as decoys—gradually being overgrown by the jungle.

For some reason, ML417 (carrying Indian serial number HS543) was passed to the Indian Air Force Museum in 1967. It was at this location that American Senator Norman Garr obtained the aircraft in 1971, having it shipped back to the United States for restoration. Work was started on the airframe and engine but little was completed.

The plane was eventually purchased by Stephen Grey and sent back to England, where Personal Plane Services did a magnificent job restoring it and reconverting it back into a single-place configuration—no small task since the entire fuselage had to be placed in a jig and the front cockpit moved back to its original location.

The rebuilt fighter, painted in splendidly accurate No. 443 (RCAF) Squadron markings, took to the air for the first time again on 10 August 1984. Since then, the Spit has been flown regularly at air shows in Britain and Europe, and played an active role in the 1988 television miniseries *Piece of Cake.*

These three survivors of the Spitfire series serve as a reminder of the deadly air battles waged across Europe and other combat fronts during a period when the Allied victory was not assured. The surviving Spitfires are nowhere near as numerous as P-51 Mustangs, but the aircraft has a graceful yet powerful form that is at least as popular wherever it is displayed.

High above a Texas cloudscape, Tiger Destefani keeps formation with Pardue in the Mk. IX.

D B

The CAF's Spitfire is equipped with an eight-gun wing. This aircraft served with three air forces.

Green Machine: the Falcon Special

Before the advent of the jet engine, aeronautical engineers who dreamed of conquering new dimensions in horizontal speed sketched out muscle plane designs that combined the absolute minimum of airframe with the absolute maximum of engine. The designs were many and varied: there were the various (and deadly) GeeBees designed and built by the Granville brothers; the more practical Wedell-Williams racers, which were at least survivable; and the sleekly art-deco Laird-Turner speed demons, along with a host of other designs—some that established new speed records and gained headlines, and others that, perhaps more finally, made just obituaries and small smoking holes in the ground.

The thirties was a decade obsessed with the concept of streamlining—a term that influenced the design of such everyday items as toasters (the flow-through Toast-A-Lator was a particularly offensive example).

Simple, homespun American ingenuity accounted for most of America's obsession with aeronautical speed. Young designers and builders across the country constructed homebuilt speed ships to compete in the prestigious Thompson and Bendix Trophy races—races in which the winner was the first aircraft to blaze across the finish line.

Many of these designs from the late twenties and thirties were inelegant and relied strictly on brute horsepower to achieve new speed records. However, some began to show real aeronautical advancement with items like cantilever wings, enclosed cockpits, retractable landing gear and tightly enclosed cowlings. The racers were capable of showing a clean pair of heels to virtually any contemporary military warplane, and the advancements of these backyard designers and pilots were not lost upon the military. Many of these improvements were quickly incorporated into the designs of the major manufacturers.

World War II put an end to air racing for the duration. During the war, some military designs followed the concept of trying to put a huge engine on a small airframe; the Focke-Wulf Fw 190 and Grumman F8F Bearcat are prime examples. Piston engine technology advanced rapidly with stunning engines like the Rolls-Royce Griffon, Wright R-3350 and Pratt & Whitney R-4360 being developed and put into service. The development of jet technology quickly made the fire-breathing piston engines obsolete, however, and after the war the public rapidly became fascinated with jets and a whole new generation of aviation record breaking.

To some aviators, the idea of mating a big engine to a small airframe is still irresistible—witness the popularity of the Reno Air Races, still going strong after more than twenty-five years. In the small gold rush town of Columbia, California, a daring new aircraft blasted into the sky for the first time in 1987—an aircraft that perhaps represented the ultimate in miniscule muscle planes.

Master woodworker Ron Cox had earlier constructed a small air show biplane called the Falcon Special and campaigned it through a number of shows, but he wanted something more. Using the basic all-wood Falcon design, Cox decided to create the ultimate mini-biplane for air show work.

continued on page 40

The Green Machine roars over a thick fog bank. This highly modified Falcon Special was billed as the world's highest-horsepower small biplane by builder and pilot Ron Cox.

LYC 0540
300+H.P

continued from page 38

The resulting airframe was absolutely flawless—the ultrasmooth fabric and wood surface a testimonial to Cox's construction abilities. Painted a brilliant hue of green ("I like green," said Cox. "Just about everything I have is green.") with yellow trim, the biplane spanned only sixteen feet from wing tip to wing tip and from nose to tail.

The small crowds of spectators at Columbia Airport were stunned by the aircraft's performance during Cox's early test flights. To get the performance he wanted, Cox installed a 300 plus horsepower Lycoming O-540 engine which had been highly modified and finely tuned for F-16 style takeoffs by Barrett Performance in Tulsa, Oklahoma. With a three-blade propeller that looked way too big for its airframe, the aircraft, named the Green Machine, was a pocket rocket. "It's the smallest biplane with the most horsepower flying," said Cox.

Because of the hazards of air show work, Cox built as many safety devices into the cockpit as possible. His own personal gear included a Nomex flight suit, gloves and a complete head mask. "Sure it's uncomfortable with that thing on but if there's an accident," said Cox, "it's going to give you a couple extra seconds to get out of the plane."

Cox installed a smoke system in the aircraft and carefully planned out a dramatic air show routine, and the Green Machine was soon in demand for air shows across the United States.

When I visited scenic Columbia Airport in December 1987 to meet Cox and photograph the biplane, I was impressed by the detail design work Cox had undertaken to make his radical midget as safe as possible. "Although it's built mainly of wood, there's a complete firewall separating the pilot from the engine," he pointed out. "It's a shame that the technology that lets Indy car drivers walk away from 200 mph wrecks can't be transferred to aircraft. Hell, we're flying around in cockpits that haven't changed in fifty years."

When we launched out of Columbia for our photo mission, it was evident that the aircraft had some stability problems. "I'm still working on a few things," said Cox. When the speed built up, the Green Machine stabilized and Cox went through some of his maneuvers. The massive power made for some mighty impressive aerobatics as the aircraft carved up the sky over the Sierra foothills.

As soon as the 1988 air show season started, Ron Cox and his wife, Cindy, were on the circuit with the Green Machine, and bookings rapidly built up as the word got out about the mighty biplane. Some pilots describe air show work as pretty routine, but the routine can be shattered by a few moments of terror. Those few moments came to Cox and the Green Machine in April 1988, while doing their routine at the huge Sun 'N Fun air show in Lakeland, Florida.

Cox was performing a spectacular inverted flat spin with the smoke on when the Green Machine suddenly caught fire. The cockpit instantly filled with smoke, and Cox lost reference to the ground. Frantically remembering his last sighting of the runway, Cox attempted to right the biplane as it slammed into the ground.

The air show crowd immediately feared the worst . . . and with good reason. The aircraft lay smashed and burning as the crash crew quickly responded, saving Cox's life.

The design work that had gone into the Green Machine paid off, and the crashworthy cockpit area did its job. Since Cox is a firm believer in

continued on page 42

Smoke on, the Green Machine comes out of a dive over Columbia, California. Having a wingspan of only 16 feet and a length of 16 feet, and powered by a modified Lycoming 0-540 of over 300 hp, the small biplane offered exceptional performance.

continued from page 40
wearing fire-resistant flight clothing, the flames did not do as much damage as they could have.

Cox was badly injured in the crash and had to spend some months in a body brace, but he recovered and a new Green Machine has flown as we go to press.

With the Sierras as a backdrop, Ron Cox rolls the Green Machine past the camera place. The biplane, which is built mainly of wood, has a superb finish, due to the fact that Ron is a professional woodworker.

GREEN
MACHINE

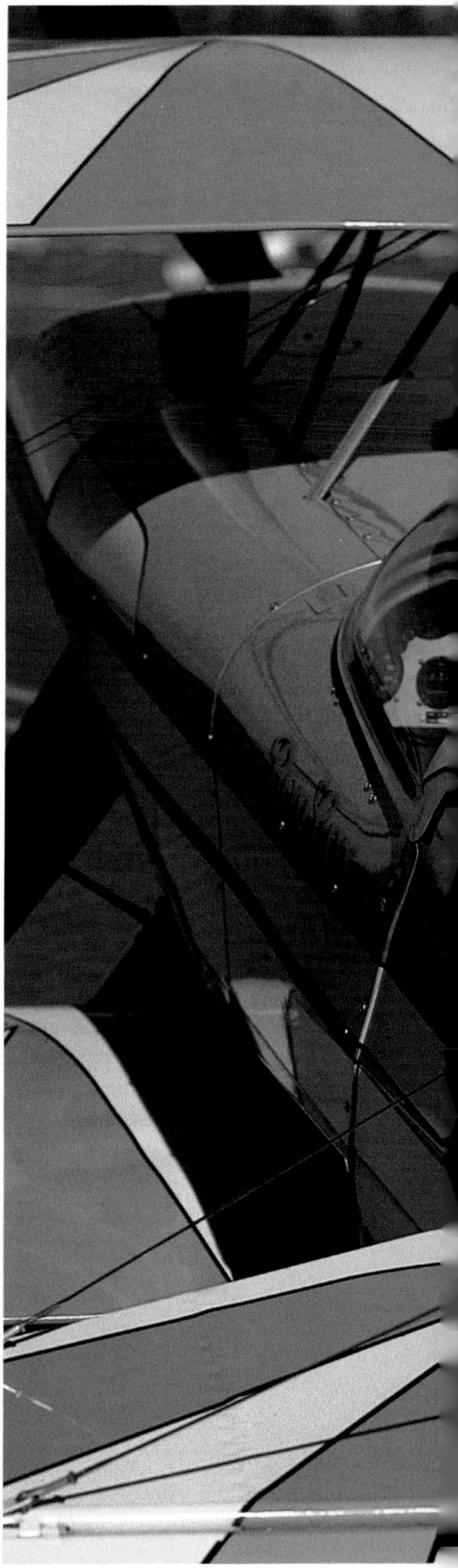

Flying inverted, this view highlights the size of the three-blade propeller when compared with the airframe.

Cox built as much crashworthiness into the Green Machine as possible—and this paid off in the Florida air show accident.

Cox used Indy race car technology to build the cockpit of the Green Machine strong enough so that he was able to survive the plane's violent crash.

Every boy should have one: North American P-51 Mustang

High over the billowing clouds obscuring the farmlands surrounding Miami, Florida, a bit of aeronautical history was making its presence known. A finely tuned Rolls-Royce/Packard Merlin roared out its magic music as Kermit Weeks looped and rolled his highly polished North American P-51D Mustang.

Mustang!

No matter what the British say about their legendary Spitfire, the Mustang was the finest fighter aircraft of World War II. This sleek fighter was created to British specifications by a designer of German training and ancestry at a new Los Angeles aircraft factory in just a few months' time! Early variants were powered with the American Allison V-12 motor, but true greatness came later when the American airframe was mated with the British Rolls-Royce V-1650 motor, eventually license-built in the United States by Packard.

After World War II, the Mustang continued to fly with many air forces and was only retired from active service in 1985, the Dominican Republic being the last air force to operate the type. Today, the Mustang is the most numerous of surviving World War II fighters; about 100 remain active. Of that number,

continued on page 50

Cripes A' Mighty 3rd *in the middle of a pack of Mustangs high above the Florida haze layer. Kermit Weeks decided his Mustang should be a natural metal finish rather than painted so that it would conform to World War II standards. The other P-51Ds in this formation are painted silver and the distinction is obvious.*

Double Trouble two
CRIPES A'MIGHTY 3RD
PETE McMANUS

Weeks and his crew went to considerable trouble to re-create the markings of ace George Preddy. Red McVay, assistant crew chief and only surviving ground crew member, aided in documenting the markings and colors.

Kermit Weeks, creator of the Weeks Air Museum, is shown here in the cockpit of his P-51D. "By installing as much original equipment as possible in the Mustang, I have set a standard by which the remainder of our museum aircraft will be restored," says Weeks.

continued from page 46
perhaps the most authentic Mustang is the one owned and operated by the Weeks Air Museum, Tamiami Airport, Florida.

The rapidly expanding Weeks Air Museum is the masterwork of well-known aerobatic pilot Kermit Weeks. In a fairly short amount of time, Weeks has built up an impressive air force of vintage planes, both military and civilian. His goal is to restore each aircraft to original condition. This means that aircraft like the Mustang will receive such authentic items as gunsights, armor plating, weapons and so on.

"This Mustang is sort of our pattern aircraft," stated Weeks, as he admired the polished metal beauty parked in the long grass at Tamiami Airport. "We restored this aircraft with the idea that it would be the guide for our other restorations."

P-51D-25-NT USAAF serial number 44-11507 rolled off North American's Dallas, Texas, production line in February 1945. The fighter was immediately earmarked for America's ally in the South Pacific, the Royal New Zealand Air Force. It was crated and shipped to New Zealand along with twenty-eight other P-51Ds, but the atomic bomb brought the war to an end before the Mustang shipment was ready for service.

Without the Japanese to fight, New Zealand had little reason for an air force, so the planes were assigned to the Territorial Air Force (a local air national guard) and were operated for just two years, from 1952 to 1954.

continued on page 51

Following pages
"Bringing an aircraft back to its original combat specifications means that its original weapons or replicas of the same must be installed," states Kermit Weeks. These realistic .50 caliber Browning air-cooled machine gun replicas were created by Kittyhawk Aviation. Note the original bore-sighting instructions inside the gun access panel.

continued from page 50
The low-time aircraft were put into storage for several years, and in 1958 the New Zealand Government Disposals Board put them up for sale to the highest bidder.

Airline pilot John MacDonald had long admired the sleek lines of the P-51 and thought it would be splendid to own such a beautiful aircraft—all he would have to do was fight off the other bidders. At the auction site, MacDonald and partner Ron Fechney were surprised to find they were the only bidders besides a few scrap dealers. Their bid of $150 allowed the partners the pick of the litter, along with a truckload of spares that included two zero-time Merlins, an extra propeller, numerous cowlings, landing gear and extra radiators.

Now that MacDonald and Fechney had the plane, they had to figure out what to do with it. The bureaucracy in New Zealand demanded that the Mustang be completely disassembled for a minute inspection, since a civil P-51 had never been operated in the country. Even though the Mustang was in good condition and had few flying hours, the owners were forced to comply with this unreasonable rule. The work was done in the hangar of New Zealand National Airways Corporation.

The aircraft was finally assigned civil registration ZK-CCG in 1964, and was then flown to Fechney's farm where it was kept in a barn and flown off a grass airstrip. Mobil Oil's logo was painted on the sides of the white and red Mustang because that company agreed to provide fuel to keep the Merlin going.

MacDonald and Fechney had put 120 flying hours on the aircraft by 1968, when the plane went inactive owing to high operating costs. The Mustang was carefully stored in the barn, and many offers from American buyers were politely fended off.

In 1973, John Schafhausen's son was visiting New Zealand and heard
continued on page 55

The finely detailed cockpit of the Mustang contains all its original 1944 equipment. The original radios have been added since this photograph was taken. The K-14 gunsight dominates the Mustang's cockpit, complete with original padding that would make some small effort in protecting the pilot's face during a crash landing. Weeks has installed an original rubberized fuel cell behind the pilot's seat, but it is nonfunctioning.

The Weeks Air Museum is currently restoring a variety of aircraft, including a Warhawk, a Corsair and a Flying Fortress—all of which will be finished to the standards of Cripes A' Mighty 3rd.

CRIPES A'MIGHTY 3RD
CHIEF-S/Sgt LEW LUNN
ASST-Cpl RED McVAY
ARM-Sgt M.G. KUHANECK

continued from page 51

the plane might be for sale. He met with the owners and relayed the information back to his father, who then tendered an offer. The offer was accepted, but negotiations were not completed until 1974.

ZK-CCG was then prepared for its final flight in New Zealand. It was ferried to the US Navy's Operation Deep Freeze base, where it was disassembled, loaded into a container and then shipped to Seattle, Washington, along with many of the spare parts that had been acquired at the surplus sale.

The Mustang arrived in October 1974 and was carefully assembled. It was finally test flown in February 1975, with John Herlihy doing the honors.

Schafhausen made a few local flights in the Mustang before he decided to ground the plane for the application of a military paint scheme. He chose the colorful markings of Major George Preddy's *Cripes A' Mighty 3rd.* The result was hailed as a new step in warbird restoration as the quest for original equipment and accuracy was just beginning during this period.

Schafhausen flew the plane for several years before selling it to Gene Stocker, who in turn sold it to Kermit Weeks. Weeks flew the Mustang around to local shows and aerobatic meets until, on a trip to the World Aerobatic contest in Wisconsin, a magneto quit on the Merlin.

First Weeks took the aircraft to Rockford, Illinois, to repair the mag, but since the V-1650-7 engine had 400 hours' operating time, he decided to remove the Merlin and send it to Zendroi Engines in Chicago for an overhaul. During the overhaul, longer-lived transport heads and banks were installed. After this rebuild, the engine

continued on page 57

Flaps and gear down, the Mustang loses a bit of its fabled sleekness but is still every inch a thoroughbred.

CRIPES A'MIGHTY 3RD

continued from page 55

was put back in the fighter. In March 1981, the plane was flown back to Florida, where it sat outside for about eight months while Weeks waited for a new hangar to become available.

As any resident of or visitor to Florida knows, the sun in the Miami area gets intense, *very* intense. It was not long before the paint on NL921 began to do strange things. It turned out that when the fighter was painted, the surfaces had been prepared with a thick layer of Bondo. The Florida sun quickly dried out the Bondo so that the paint began to crack and peel, with corrosion quickly taking hold on the areas of exposed metal.

During this time, Weeks flew NL921 fairly regularly. He was going to take the plane to the annual Oshkosh show when the starter clutch went out. He had also been having oil pressure problems with the Merlin, so he sent the motor back to Zendroi for further work and took his Curtiss P-40E Kittyhawk to Oshkosh instead.

Kermit Weeks and Kent McMakin had just completed an extensive restoration of a Grumman Duck when the Mustang was rolled into the restoration shop. The plane was disassembled and work began. McMakin and Sam Taber worked long and hard on the Mustang, while Weeks did a lot of the machining work and Linda Meyers aided the project wherever possible.

The inside of the aircraft was found to be almost military stock; about the only items that had been removed—aside from all the stuff in the rear cockpit that had to go to

continued on page 58

On 6 August 1944, George Preddy, suffering from a deadly hangover, took the 352nd Fighter Group for a mission to Germany. Even though he was sick through much of the flight, Preddy managed to do the almost impossible: He destroyed six Messerschmitt Me 109s and was awarded the Distinguished Service Cross, America's second-highest award for valor.

continued from page 57
make way for the rear seat—were the guns and gun mounts. All the original armament wiring was still in place, as were most of the other military bits and pieces. Even the panel and side consoles were almost stock.

"Once we got into the aircraft, we went further than we had anticipated," commented McMakin, who heads up the restoration shop for the Weeks Air Museum. "The Duck had been our first aircraft, but the Mustang defined how we would do our future projects. We eventually decided to go in-depth into the aircraft and bring the Mustang back to as stock condition as possible. We decided to put the guns and ammo back in . . . everything would be just like World War II."

After all the paint and Bondo had been stripped off, the crew was not at all pleased to find that an orbital sander had been used on the entire airframe, scarring and cutting every bit of metal. The crew had planned to paint the plane silver overall and apply the markings over the paint. As an experiment, however, McMakin and Taber simply began polishing a piece of metal. Measuring the metal before and after polishing, they discovered that only a small bit of aluminum had been removed in the process. Since a polished aircraft would look much more authentic than a painted one, they decided to go ahead and polish the entire airframe. They might not have made that decision if they had known that the polishing would take the two of them, along with a part-time assistant, two months! But the results were well worth the effort.

Other than the sanding, the airframe metal was in good condition—with two exceptions. One, part of the wing leading edge had to be replaced because the Royal New Zealand Air Force had installed a patch to cover some damage. Although it was neatly done, the patch would be too conspicuous with the bare metal finish. And two, John Neel of Griffin, Georgia, completely redid the fairings for the wing and tail, making the dented units look just like new.

The markings were carefully applied with the aid of Sam Sox and Joe Noah along with Joe "Red" McVay, assistant crew chief on Preddy's plane and the only surviving member of the ground crew. The authentic markings were achieved through months of research and the minute study of old photographs and documents.

Finally, Brian O'Farrell helped acquire a few stock items that were needed to complete the machine, and Kittyhawk Aviation at Chino, California, manufactured a beautiful set of six replica .50 caliber Browning machine guns. Weeks decided to install the rear fuselage tank, but the original tank in the museum had become brittle and the bottom had to be cut out so it would fit into the area behind the pilot. Atop this, the restorers added an original radio rack directly behind the armor plate (original radios were installed after the photos in this text were taken). A K-14 gunsight gave the cockpit that final look of military authenticity.

The Mustang was assembled in June and July of 1986, and the first flight after restoration was on 28 January 1987. "It was kinda scary," said Weeks. "Everything worked the first time out and, besides the usual minor adjustments, we did not have to do one thing."

Weeks and his crew should feel proud of their magnificent Mustang. More important, they have put down the ground rules for further restorations at the Weeks Air Museum—a museum that will certainly have a fine collection of beautifully rebuilt aircraft for future generations to study and admire.

High over the ocean, Weeks sets the Mustang up into landing configuration. This view shows the high polish of this Mustang's aluminum skin.

HO
CRIPES A'MIGHTY 3RD

Thunder from Port Alberni: Martin Mars

From 1,000 feet above, the water of Sproat Lake appears almost black—with just a touch of blue. At the near end of the lake, the surface is placid, forming an onyx mirror that reflects the blue sky and puffy white clouds. At the far end of the lake, a prehistoric-appearing behemoth moves forward on the surface, leaving a churning, roiling wake of water in its passage.

Scenic Sproat Lake is located on equally scenic Vancouver Island, just across a stretch of water from the bustling modern city in British Columbia that bears the same name. This long lake is home to the Loch Ness Monsters of Vancouver Island: the last two Martin Mars flying boats, which are also the last two four-engine piston-powered flying boats still actively operating. Thousands of visitors are drawn each year to catch sight of the ultimate muscle planes as they bask in the sun at their water-based tie-downs or thunder into the air to do battle with human's oldest enemy: fire.

Back on the lake, the red and white behemoth suddenly takes on a new purpose. Chief Captain Jack Waddington smoothly but purposefully advances the large throttles mounted on a pedestal in the center of the spacious cockpit. With power fully applied, the Mars comes alive, rising up in the water as the

continued on page 62

Thirty tons of fire-suppressing water roar out of the hull of the Philippine Mars *during a practice fire drop. Forest Industries Flying Tankers' philosophy is to kill a fire as soon as it's spotted, and few developing fires can stand up to an onslaught from the Mars.*

PHILIPPINE MARS

continued from page 60
throttles come forward. A huge bow wave begins to form off the giant hull as acceleration increases. The roaring radials cause flocks of birds to rise from the forests surrounding the lake. In the small town of Port Alberni, at the east end of the lake, knowing smiles are exchanged among citizens. The Mars is going to work.

Waddington concentrates on keeping the craft straight and level during the takeoff run. Copilot John de Bourcier assists Waddington while observing the instruments and keeping an eye open for floating logs or other waterborne debris that could impede the Mars' charge toward flight. Back under wing, the flight engineer monitors his engine instruments to make sure the Wrights are running as advertised.

Suddenly, gracefully, the Mars detaches itself from the water. The boat becomes an airplane—a magnificent airplane, the last survivor of a glorious period in aviation history.

On land, at the seaplane ramp, Tom Irving watches the takeoff, using his hands to shade his eyes against the bright sun. "Looks good. Yeah, there they go," says Irving, as the Mars gains altitude.

Irving is the director of Forest Industries Flying Tankers (FIFT) and is the man responsible for the care, feeding and operation of the two flying boats. FIFT is owned and operated by a consortium of Canadian logging companies, and the two vintage ex-military aircraft are used to protect the extensive forest holdings of the companies.

Forest products are the major industry in the area, and fast-moving blazes can destroy valuable resources and put people out of work. The flying boats are there to stop that threat. Irving states the utility of the Mars simply: "The Mars costs about $2,500 (Canadian) to operate per hour. Some full-grown lumber trees are worth that amount . . . individually."

The first Martin Mars had twin vertical tails and a lot of other different features from those on the surviving aircraft. Designated XPB2M-1, it was originally created as a long-range patrol bomber, first flying in June 1942. The Mars never became operational as a patrol bomber, however. It was instead converted to a transport, and it faithfully performed this role through the war.

The US government ordered twenty improved variants of the Mars, but this order was cut back to six following the end of the war. One aircraft sank following a test flight and another was destroyed by fire, but four were delivered to the Navy as JRM-ls in 1946.

The Mars transport flew between NAS Alameda (near San Francisco) and Hawaii—flights averaging 11½ to 14½ hours depending on the wind. It performed the transport role with efficiency, but there was just not much need for huge flying boats. Martin dropped the idea of building an airline version of the Mars, and in 1959 the Navy finally retired the fleet, which now included a single JRM-2 powered by Pratt & Whitney R-4360 radials.

The Mars is a giant aircraft. Its wing spans 200 feet (the length of an average city block), and its vertical tail rises forty-eight feet (about the height of a four-story building). Its length is 120 feet and its gross weight is 162,000 lb. The two Mars converted for water bombing can carry 7,000 gallons of water, weighing 60,000 lb., aloft.

When the transports became available for surplus sale, Dan MacIvor, chief pilot for the Macmillin Bloedel timber company, immediately saw the value of the aircraft as protectors of the company's resources.

continued on page 67

Trailing a vestigial stream of water following a drop, the Mars prepares to enter a 30 degree bank to the right in a climbing turn away from the drop zone.

Hand on the throttle quadrant, Philippine Mars *chief captain Jack Waddington prepares for a training flight.*

With an engine out, the Mars climbs away from the lake on which the crew has been practicing takeoffs with an engine failure. The vintage Wright radials have proven reliable.

continued from page 62
He broached the idea to his bosses, and after some serious planning, the four aircraft were purchased along with a huge quantity of spare parts, including thirty vital R-3350 engines.

The planes were flown to Vancouver Island and conversion work was started to turn the aircraft into water bombers. A simple modification was made by installing a fiberglass and wood water tank in the fuselage, along with four large doors on the side of the fuselage, which could be triggered to drop the water load. This caused a minimum of damage to the airframe in case the idea did not work and the planes had to be converted back to the transport role and sold. But the concept did work, and of the last conversion incorporated more efficient doors located in the bottom of the hull.

The first aircraft to be converted was the *Marianas Mars,* followed by the *Philippine Mars* in 1962. Unfortunately, the *Caroline Mars* was damaged that year in a windstorm and the plane was scrapped. ("If we knew that the program was going to be so successful and the aircraft would operate so long, we never would have scrapped that aircraft. We would have rebuilt it," said Tom Irving.) The *Hawaii Mars* was the last aircraft to be completed; it was the one fitted with the water-dropping chutes in the bottom of the hull.

FIFT went to work learning about the Mars and about how best to use it in firefighting. Maneuvering the plane close to the ground takes skill and forethought. Water bombing is a dangerous job; flying in smoke, superheated air and mountainous terrain all have their special hazards—and this truth was underscored with the loss of the *Marianas Mars* with all its crew during the early phase of the Mars program.

The accident was a serious blow to FIFT, but operations had to continue. As a safety measure, it was decided to use a Grumman Goose as a bird dog for Mars operations. The twin-engine Goose would lead the Mars to the target and would be flown by a Mars captain who knew the characteristics and limitations of the water dropper. This arrangement has worked out extremely well, and the two remaining bombers have had accident-free records during nearly thirty years of continuous operation.

The Mars captains that fly for FIFT are an experienced bunch of bush pilots with lots of water-flying time. "I always wanted to be a pilot," said Waddington. "I drove a gas truck at the airport then started flying small float planes like the Cessna 180/5 series then went on to Beavers, Otters, Gooses, etc. In 1975 there was a vacancy and I joined the company. There's a three-year check-out on the Mars and I was overwhelmed with my first flight in the plane. It's slow, big and cumbersome. The rudder and elevator are boosted but the ailerons are manual and it really takes some muscle to get that thing turning. We require a new pilot to have a minimum of 3,000 hours of water flying time. Our Mars pilots average 10,000 hours. We have established a very safe operational procedure for operating the Mars. All flying is strictly by procedure."

During fire season, one Mars usually takes a leisurely morning cruise down Sproat Lake and then heads back to its anchorage near the base's pier. The taxi run warms up the engine oil, which will stay hot enough for the remainder of the day in case the plane needs to scramble to a fire. If the second Mars is needed, it will warm up its engines while taxiing.

Fire scrambles are amazingly efficient. When the siren sounds, the crew either is in the plane or reaches

continued on page 68

If the day comes when the Wright R-3350 supply dries up or overhauls become impossible, FIFT has carried out an extensive engineering survey and plans to replace the motors with Allison turboprops.

continued from page 67

the plane quickly by motorboat from the dock. The R-3350s kick over easily, and in a cloud of blue exhaust smoke, the Mars begins to move forward. As power increases, the Mars gets on its step and lifts off between eighty and ninety knots. Usually, the first Mars is empty and will immediately head to a nearby lake for a pickup. The second Mars will also scoop water on its takeoff run and head directly to the fire.

Water is picked up by skimming the surface of one of the many lakes in the area. Constant communication is kept with the Goose, whose pilot is also talking to ground personnel, if any are present. The captain brings the Mars down to seventy knots while the copilot operates the flaps. Power settings are done by the flight engineer. Two probes are lowered from the hull, and the 7,000 gallons of water are uplifted in twenty to thirty seconds. The probes retract, and the flight engineer brings up the power (each engine is rated at 2500 hp maximum) to get the Mars off the water.

"During our run on a fire," said Waddington, "the pilot handles the controls while the copilot does the throttles. He takes care of all throttle settings during the drop."

During the drop, the Mars is usually at a height of between 100 and 150 feet and a speed of about 120 knots. Once over the fire, the captain releases the water at the appropriate moment, while the first officer opens up the throttles to give the captain the needed power to climb up and away, and head for another pickup. The average time for replenishment between drops is about fifteen minutes, much better than with land-based fire bombers. Each load of

continued on page 70

Gracefully skimming the surface of a lake, the Mars takes on its full load of 7,000 gallons of water.

PHILIPPINE MARS

continued from page 68
water can cover an area 600 feet by 200 feet.

The effect of thirty tons of water cascading on a blaze can hardly be imagined. Trees are broken in two, vegetation is uprooted—but, usually, the fire is killed. "We don't want to surround, contain and then knock out the fire like some governmental agencies prefer," said Irving. "We want to kill the fire . . . immediately."

Since the Mars flying boats have been introduced to forest-fire-fighting duties, the amount of timber destroyed each year has been drastically lowered. The men and women of FIFT are a dedicated group that clearly love their big boats. During the off-season (the aircraft are made operational on 15 April each year), much work and repair goes into each Mars.

The future? An engineering survey has been undertaken that will allow the Mars to be fitted with Allison turboprops if the supply of Wright radials runs out. It would not be impossible for these aircraft to operate for another forty to fifty years.

For now? The two red and white Mars rock gently back and forth on the placid water to Sproat Lake, waiting to do battle with man's oldest enemy.

"We're number one!" indicates Jack Waddington as the Mars thunders through another practice run. The Mars usually carries a crew of four during active fire drops.

INE MARS

The last interceptor: Convair F-106 Delta Dart

It was an offer I could not refuse. In preparing this volume, I had the chance to fly in lots of unusual aircraft, but one of my big thrills was getting airborne in the mighty Convair F-106B—not just once, but twice, as I took photographs for the swan song of the last of America's famed "Century Series" fighters.

I was getting just about the last media ride in the 106 with the 119th Fighter Interceptor Squadron, 177th Fighter Group, of the New Jersey Air National Guard—or, as the unit is more popularly known, "The Jersey Devils." There I was, strapped into the back seat of one of the 119th's immaculate two-seat B-model Delta Darts, encumbered with immersion suit, flight suit, G-suit, parachute and, of course, helmet and oxygen mask.

Up in the pointed end, Major Ralph Omann was going through the last of his preflight checks, occasionally glancing back to make sure I wasn't doing anything embarrassing—or dangerous. We took the active at Atlantic City, New Jersey, a relatively rural airport that caters to both civilian and military traffic—away from the neon glitter of the new gambling casinos rising high above the town's skyline.

Major Omann lined up with the white stripe painted down the

continued on page 75

Old and new fly together. The powerful form of an F-106A is accompanied by the smaller F-16A Fighting Falcon during the 120th Fighter Interceptor Group's transition to the General Dynamics air superiority fighter.

671
Montana
72482
Big Sky Country
U.S. AIR FORCE
12

U.S. AIR FORCE
USAF

Streaming two trails of high-grade kerosene, Captain Tony Sobrero heads straight for the moon. The F-106A had a combat range of 365 miles and could climb to 51,000 feet in just under seven minutes.

continued from page 72

runway's centerline, popped the brakes and let the F-106B lurch ahead as he jammed the throttle forward. The 32,000 plus pounds of aircraft began to rumble down the long runway—until Major Omann shoved the throttle up through a lock and into full afterburner. Acceleration suddenly took on a new meaning as the Pratt & Whitney J75-P-17 spat out 24,500 pounds of pure thrust. Century Series fighters were ground lovers, but in afterburner the 106 quickly ate up its alloted section of runway and became gracefully airborne, its dramatic delta wings contrasting strangely with the rural countryside.

The Convair F-106 Delta Dart, which joined the Air Defense Command in May 1959, was feted as the first USAF fighter to achieve twenty years of operational service, and it came close to making the thirty-year mark—an almost unheard of record for an operational combat aircraft. This distinction would compare to having an operational 1944 Boeing B-17G Flying Fortress sitting ready to go on a Strategic Air Command ramp sometime during 1974!

Clearly, the USAF got good value for its money with the Delta Dart. The unit cost for the F-106A was $4.7 million, a price that was probably expensive by late-fifties' standards but that seems more than reasonable today. (As an example, it has been estimated that the unit cost for the new Advanced Tactical Fighter might be in excess of $100 million!)

The Convair F-106 was America's last purpose-built interceptor. It was originally developed as an advanced follow-up to the F-102 Delta Dagger and designated F-102B, but the design was so different from the earlier interceptor that the designation was changed to F-106A.

Seventeen test examples were ordered from Convair on 28 April 1955. The modern interceptor would be powered by the Pratt & Whitney J75-P-17 and would carry the remarkably advanced Hughes MA-1 fire control system.

The MA-1 was linked directly with the extensive SAGE ground control system, which was tied into the DEW (Distant Early Warning) system. The mating of these systems allowed the interceptor to be flown automatically from just after becoming airborne to just before landing. Military planners felt this would lead to a more efficient interceptor force against Soviet bombers. The pilot would be able to watch over the entire mission on a map read-out display and take over the controls any time he felt it was necessary to assume command of the mission.

Armament for the F-106A was also interesting. Remember, this aircraft was designed in an era when the airborne gun was considered obsolete and the missile was the new king of aerial warfare. The F-106A was built to tote the AIR-2A Genie air-to-air missile into combat, along with four Falcon radar homing missiles.

The Genie was one of those great misconceived ideas from the Fabulous Fifties. The reasoning was that a large air-to-air missile equipped with a nuclear warhead would be just the thing for breaking up Russian bomber formations as they battled their way south. Apparently little thought was given to the friendly (probably Canadian) citizens underneath the flight path and what the Genie would do to them! Furthermore, the Genie was unguided; at the time, guidance systems were rather imprecise, so military planners decided a nuclear

continued on page 77

Montana
72482
Big Sky Country
U.S. AIR FOR
12

continued from page 75

knockout punch would be easier to achieve than accuracy and precision.

Be this as it may, the Genie was reckoned to be a powerful and advanced weapon for its day (although the Montana Air National Guard's Northrop F-89 Scorpion "gate guardian" was the only aircraft to fire an armed Genie during operational testing). One New Jersey National Guard 106 pilot stated, "You're dead wrong. Russian bombers, with their advanced ECM systems, are getting harder and harder to find, much less destroy. The unguided Genie gave us a real edge and I was sorry to see it go when the weapon was phased out of service a few years ago."

Convair test pilot Richard Johnson took the prototype 106 aloft on 26 December 1956, and the first production aircraft joined the Air Defense Command (ADC) in May 1959. Construction of the F-106 took place at Convair's factory in San Diego, California. The company was contracted for 277 single-seat F-106As and sixty-three two-place F-106Bs. The last Delta Dart was delivered to ADC on 20 July 1961.

Over the years, many modifications were introduced to make the interceptors more effective. When the airborne gun came back into style, some Darts had the reliable M-61 20 mm Vulcan rotary cannon fitted neatly into the forward portion of the weapon bay. Avionics and fire control systems were updated, and a clear-view canopy was added (this was needed when dogfighting came back into style during the Vietnam War). One of several experimental modifications included work on making the 106 into a tri-motor (two

continued on page 78

A classic portrait of a classic fighter soaring high over the Montana mountains. Only 277 F-106As and 63 two-seat F-106Bs were produced by Convair's factory in San Diego, California.

continued from page 77
additional engines would be hung under the wing) that would boost the plane's top speed past the Mach 3 mark.

The Montana ANG's F-106s were "old style," while The Jersey Devils's F-106s were fitted with clear-view canopies, digital instruments and the internal 20 mm Vulcan cannon. The fitting of digital instruments made a new check-out mandatory for 106 jocks who transferred from "round" Darts (those equipped with the more traditional style instruments). "Oddly enough," said one New Jersey ANG pilot, "that instrument change made flying the 106 a whole new ball of wax."

Even though the F-106 was a limited production aircraft, it saw extensive use among USAF interceptor squadrons. When phased out of active service, it found a brand-new life with the Air National Guard.

"Our aircraft were a bit rough when we received them from the regulars," stated a Montana ANG crew chief who had been with his Dart for fourteen years. "It took us awhile, but we really got the Darts fine-tuned for our mission." A view of the Montana ramp and spotless main hangar proved this statement to be true. Each vintage interceptor was groomed to a fine state. It was difficult, if not impossible, to find an aircraft with chipped paint or grease stains.

Individual Montana touches included painting the cockpit interiors a light shade of blue. "We heard that the new Russian fighters had their interiors painted light blue so we tried it on our birds," said one crew chief (perhaps with more whimsey than for any tactical reason).

continued on page 80

The F-106B passes over the camera plane. Even though the two-seater was used mainly for training and indoctrination, the B-model was fully combat capable.

New
Jersey
90155

continued from page 78

One Dart was heavily damaged after flipping over on the runway. Rather than scrap the plane, the Montana maintenance troops painstakingly re-created the entire forward section of the aircraft (parts were almost impossible to come by) and returned the interceptor to service. Close observation showed a slightly different nose contour . . . the only difference in an amazing project that brought a Dart back from the scrap heap and into active service.

Montana's glossy gray interceptor paint schemes have given way to the drab gray camouflage of the F-16s, and the colorful blue bands are no more. The Montana ANG crew chiefs were sad to see their aircraft go, "but we'll put the F-16s in the same shape," they said—and they did. One enlisted man designed a most effective insignia for the vertical tail, giving the Fighting Falcons from Montana a most distinctive look as they continue their important air defense mission.

When the New Jersey ANG phased out its Darts in June 1988 and removed from active service the last of the Century Series fighters, a significant era in military aviation came to an end. A lavish party was staged for the event.

The New Jersey ANG's 119th Fighter Interceptor Squadron, 177th Fighter Group was assigned to the Air Defense Command and equipped with the F-106A in 1973, and enjoyed an enviable record with the type from that point on. The unit is now equipped with the F-16A for the air defense role, although some pilots wish they had an aircraft with a bit more muscle.

continued on page 81

Easily read digital instruments on this New Jersey ANG F-106B show the aircraft passing 250 knots at 7,000 feet while at 97 percent engine power. The large hole atop the panel is where the scope was removed for the photographic mission.

continued from page 80

And what of the surviving Darts? As of this writing, Flight Systems, Mojave, California, has converted a small batch of the delta wing classics to target drones. The drones are undergoing flight testing with the view of converting the rest of the fleet, which is currently in storage at Davis-Monthan Air Force Base (AFB) in Arizona.

Curiously, the Montana ANG maintains an alert base at Davis-Monthan, where two F-16As are kept on immediate ready status. Just a short distance away sit the unit's former Delta Darts, baking in desert storage. "It's sorta strange," commented one ex-Dart pilot now flying Falcons. "Here we are flying the F-16s while our old Darts seem to be keeping watch on us as they sit in the boneyard."

The power cart is plugged in while a Delta Dart receives some maintenance on the Atlantic City ramp. The New Jersey ANG fighters were kept operational up until the moment of final withdrawal, June 1988.

The flying dump truck: Douglas Skyraider

One of the hardest-hitting combat aircraft of the Korean and Vietnam Wars had a very inauspicious birth—in a Washington, DC hotel room. When the US Navy entered World War II on 7 December 1941, carrier bombing aircraft were divided into two distinct categories: two-seat scout bombers and three-seat torpedo bombers. Douglas Aircraft Company controlled the majority of USN aircraft in these categories by producing the SBD Dauntless (scout bomber) and TBD Devastator (torpedo bomber). The Devastator was a disaster, quickly being slaughtered by advancing Japanese forces, but the Dauntless accrued a considerable string of victories—even though the 1930s design was rather dated.

Although Douglas enjoyed an enviable association with the Navy, company officials could sense hot new competition from Grumman and Curtiss with their Avenger and Helldiver designs. Accordingly, the company developed the XSB2D-1 and XTB2D-1 to provide new aircraft for the traditional roles. However, Douglas suffered a major blow when the Navy, through rapidly gained combat experience, changed its mind about the role of carrier-based bombers. The Bureau of Aeronautics decided that a large single-seat aircraft should be developed that would efficiently perform both missions, thus reducing the number of types in service and eliminating the need for training large numbers of extra aircrew.

In an attempt to satisfy the Navy's new requirements, Douglas designed the BTD-1, a large and ungainly looking machine. The Navy ordered 623 aircraft in early 1944 but this order was cut back and canceled after only twenty-eight examples were built. The Navy felt that new prototypes being built by Curtiss, Martin and Kaiser-Fleetwings would outperform the Douglas design in all respects.

In order to stay in the running with the Navy, Chief Aerodynamicist Gene Root, Chief Designer Leo Devlin, and Chief Engineer Ed Heinemann burned the midnight oil in their hotel room to create a design that the Navy would accept. The next day, the Navy liked what they saw but saddled Douglas with a tough set of requirements. The new aircraft, the XBT2D-1, had to be completed in the same timeframe as the prototypes from the other three companies—some of which had been ordered up to six months earlier!

Douglas agreed to the tough requirements and the Navy issued a contract for fifteen of the new single-seat bombers.

Back in California at the El Segundo factory, design and construction of a mock-up began almost immediately. The goal was to have a flying aircraft in less than one year, but other designers on the project thought this was an overly ambitious goal. The mock-up began to take form, and as it did, an entirely new era of naval bombing aircraft began to emerge.

The XBT2D-1 was big—it had to be in order to lift the loads required by the Navy. The low wing was loaded with pylons to carry a variety

continued on page 85

Firepower in formation: two AD-4Ns, one EA-1E and an AD-4 are the majority of the surviving airworthy Skyraiders in America. Several more examples are airworthy in Britain and France, and a couple more airframes are undergoing restoration in the US.

B
168
PENSACOLA
35178
178
JC
26997
409
USS INTREPID
NAVY
E
04
AK
24156
E
USS INTREPID
NAVY
VA-176
NX91935
AD4-N
124156

409
409

continued from page 82
of weapons. And the pilot sat high atop the deep fuselage, his position giving excellent visibility. The tight engine cowling held the new and powerful Wright R-3350 radial and the wings had four built-in 20 mm cannon for a very heavy punch. The mock-up was frantically completed and the Navy inspectors liked what they saw. The plane was big but, at the same time, had a graceful sense of proportion.

Constant minor revisions were made as the first XBT2D-1 neared completion. Range had to be increased along with load. Armor protection had to be added but, at the same time, weight needed to be reduced. Douglas, attempting to outdo the efforts of their competitors, used Corsair landing gear and an R-3350 of lesser horsepower in order to speed construction of the prototype. All the effort by the employees worked because when the prototype was completed in March 1945, only one of the competitors' aircraft had gotten into the air.

First flight was achieved on 18 March 1945, ahead of schedule by several months. Flight testing proceeded fairly smoothly and the Navy liked what they saw, placing an order for over 500 aircraft in May 1945. The BT2D-1 was given the name Dauntless II in order to carry on the illustrious heritage of the earlier Douglas product.

With the nuclear bombing of Japan and early conclusion of World War II, orders for the new Douglas product were drastically cut back. In April 1946, the Navy simplified its aircraft designation system with the BT2D-1 becoming the AD-1. Also, the name Dauntless II was dropped, and a new name, Skyraider, adopted.

Even though production was at a slower pace than Douglas desired, orders for new aircraft kept coming in and more Skyraiders were dispersed to operational Navy attack (VA) squadrons where pilots were quite enthusiastic about their new mounts.

By early 1950, almost 900 Skyraiders had been accepted for service by the Navy and the planes were operating off carriers all over the world. The end of World War II had seen massive cutbacks in defense-related items; huge fleets of combat aircraft were scrapped in the period of a few months. America's aerial fleet—the largest and most powerful in history—was rapidly reduced to the point of near ineffectiveness. Douglas was lucky in that orders for the Skyraider kept coming in, and its combat career was soon to begin.

On 25 June 1950, South Korea was invaded by combined North Korean forces in an attack that took the United States and its United Nations allies by complete surprise. The communist forces rapidly rolled south, pushing back Republic of Korea and American troops in a series of stinging and costly defeats.

In order to stem the red tide, the Navy, USAF and Marines threw all their aircraft into combat. The planes were a mixed lot—many World War II veterans were still operational with the military (Corsairs, Mustangs and Invaders) while the new jets were rapidly becoming operational (Sabres, Shooting Stars and Thunderjets) alongside the older veterans.

On 3 July, Skyraiders from VA-55 (operating off the USS *Valley Forge*) hit the enemy hard for the first time during an assault on Pyongyang. The enemy did not have an aircraft remotely approaching the capabilities of the Skyraider and were stunned to see the seemingly endless stream of bombs, rockets and napalm launched from the wings of the AD-1s. Once the external loads were dispensed, Skyraider pilots roared back to the target to continue their raid of devastation with withering blasts of fire from 20 mm cannon. The enemy had gotten their first taste of Skyraider power and this was just the beginning.

During the Korean War, the Navy and Marines would operate twenty-one Skyraider squadrons from carriers and land bases. The aircraft quickly gaining a reputation for reliability and accuracy. Skyraider pilots even met and defeated enemy fighters—a role for which the aircraft had never been designed. Skyraiders proved particularly useful in working with ground troops, taking out armor or gun emplacements that were holding up Allied advances. With their immense duration and heavy combat load, Skyraiders could orbit for hours—waiting to hit the enemy where it hurt most.

During the Korean War, orders for the versatile attack aircraft soared and Douglas was kept busy churning out the warplane. Skyraiders were modified and built for a wide variety of duties including airborne early warning, anti-submarine warfare, target towing, drones and drone directors. During a twelve-year production run, Douglas built 3,180 Skyraiders.

Jets were the big thing by the mid-1950s and the Skyraider's mission was supplemented by the new Douglas A4D Skyhawk jet attack bomber. A considerable body of military thinking felt that the day of the piston-engine warplane was over. They were wrong.

Throughout the 1950s, the Skyraider soldiered on with the US Navy and Marines, faithfully performing the duties required. Minor hot spots flared up around the world and Skyraiders were usually on hand to take care of business, undertaking strikes against rebel uprisings or communist incursions—even knocking down two intruding Chinese fighters during a search mission for survivors

continued on page 88

With a full weapon load aboard, Jay Cullum shows off the underside of his Skyraider. Priced much lower than a P-51D Mustang, with engine parts more readily available, the Skyraider—while not exactly economical to operate—makes for a fairly practical Warbird. "You just have to watch out for all that oil when getting in and out of the cockpit," says Cullum.

Jack Spanich was responsible for importing four ex-Armee de l'Air Skyraiders into the States during the late 1970s. He had AD-4NA NX91945, BuNo 126882, very nicely restored in USAF Vietnam War camouflage and markings and regularly visited air shows across the country. Tragically, Spanich and his wife died in this aircraft when it impacted with a mountain near Culpepper, Virginia, on 4 November 1984, while flying low to avoid bad weather.

A modest show of some of the heavy-hitting weaponry capable of being carried into combat by the Skyraider. During the Vietnam War, very serious consideration was given to re-opening the Skyraider production line since the vintage warplane was performing such sterling service above the steaming jungles of Southeast Asia.

continued from page 85

of an airliner crash in the South China Sea.

Perhaps the greatest triumph for the Skyraider was to come during the early 1960s when an ugly, brooding conflict in Southeast Asia escalated into what would become known as the Vietnam War.

By the early 1960s, the Skyraider was not really considered a front-line aircraft when it was put to work in the dank skies of Southeast Asia, but battlefield commanders quickly began to clamor for more Skyraiders. Operating from Navy carriers, Skyraiders flew mission after mission against targets in South and North Vietnam. Unlike the fuel-gulping jets, the Skyraider could stay overhead for hours on enemy targets, hitting them again and again. "The Skyraider would run out of oil before it would run out of gas," said one A-1 pilot . . . and he wasn't kidding. The range of the A-1 was limited by the Wright's thirst for oil rather than fuel. Skyraiders became heroes to airmen shot down by enemy fire as the attack aircraft circled overhead to guide in rescue helicopters and then devastate the countryside if the enemy put in an appearance.

Amazingly, Skyraiders even took on enemy MiGs. Four A-1s from VA-25 destroyed one MiG-17 and damaged another in aerial combat on 20 June 1965. The Navy flew its last combat sortie with the type in February 1968 but the Skyraider's operational days were far from over.

The USAF began receiving overhauled former USN A-1s in 1962 to train South Vietnamese Air Force pilots, and more aircraft soon began arriving to fulfill a variety of combat missions, including operations with the 1st Air Commando Wing. Like the USN, the USAF scored great successes with the A-1. But losses increased as the enemy's anti-aircraft equipment bacame more effective. Many A-1s were transferred to the South Vietnamese Air Force, but the number of airworthy airframes was steadily decreasing since it had been out of production since 1957. The military gave lots of thought to reopening the Skyraider production line, but this was never done.

The unsuccessful conclusion of the Vietnam War was also the end of the Skyraider in US military service. When South Vietnam was overrun, the forces of the North captured many intact Skyraiders and tons of spares.

Skyraiders had been sold to Britain and France during the 1950s, and the French examples saw a great deal of combat operations in Algeria and other rebeling French colonies. The American forces tried to buy back surplus French machines during the 1960s for use in Vietnam but that country, remembering its own inglorious defeat in Southeast Asia, refused to sell—causing a temporary rift between the two governments.

Some surplus British machines went to Sweden for use as target tugs while the French transferred aircraft to Cambodia, the Central African Republic and Chad.

The Vietnam War used up the majority of American Skyraiders, and surplus examples stored at the vast Davis-Monthan AFB were usually pretty well stripped to provide parts for operational machines. However,

continued on page 90

Atlanta, Georgia, warbird collector Dave Forrest spent years piecing together the hulk of AD-4 N23827 before it emerged from his hangar in mint condition. Finished in the glossy sea blue camouflage of the Atlanta Naval Air Reserve (NAR), it was one of the first totally restored Skyraiders on the warbird circuit when it appeared in the late 1970s. The AD-4 was built in larger numbers than any other Skyraider variant, appearing in eight different versions. Douglas built 372 "straight" AD-4s before diversifying to other variants. Powered by a Wright R-3350-26WA of 2700 hp, the AD-4 has a maximum speed of 320 mph at 15,000 ft. and had a maximum weight of 24,200 lb. in combat configuration.

168

continued from page 88
several American pilots realized the importance of the machine and began restoring abandoned hulks, hoping to create flying examples for the rapidly growing warbird market.

In the mid-1970s, about a half dozen former French Armee de l'Air machines were imported to America and put back to flying shape—some going on the air show circuit while a couple of others went to work as Army target tugs. Since then, several more Skyraiders have been restored to flying shape and are now popular attractions at air shows, where they serve as graphic reminders of America's many heroic battles in Korea and Southeast Asia. Between six and eight Skyraiders are currently flying in the United States, four more are airworthy in France, and a couple are undergoing restoration in Britain. There are rumors that the government of Vietnam would be happy to trade their captured examples for US dollars but these sales are being held up by the State Department. All in all, the future of the "flying dump truck from Douglas" looks most healthy as interest in the Korean and Vietnam Wars continues to grow.

EA-1E N62446 is unique in the fact that it was the last Skyraider to operate with the US Navy, being used for aeromedical testing at NAS Pensacola.

178

Round-engine rodeo: Corsair and Wildcat, Avenger and Bearcat

The west Texas town of Breckenridge, population 7,000, is located in oil country—a landscape of gently rolling hills dotted with oil wells. It is also the site of Stephens County Airport.

Now, this airport could be just like hundreds of other small regional airfields across America: a few tin hangars, a handful of Cessnas and Pipers, a gas pump and, perhaps, a flying serivce. But Stephens County breaks the mold. Passersby are likely to see a Corsair (or a Wildcat, or a Bearcat, or an Avenger, or . . .) roar overhead, shattering the country silence with the demanding roar of a huge radial engine at full power. The reason for this strange sight? Well, Breckenridge is home to Howard Pardue and the Breckenridge Air Museum.

For such a small town, Breckenridge has a disproportionate number of muscle planes—World War II warbirds lovingly restored and operated by a dedicated band of owners. The open country and lack of controlled airspace means that these aircraft are exercised often and regularly; low passes and aerobatics, with bright white trails of smoke carving up the blue Texas sky, are the order of the day.

Howard Pardue, Jimmie McMillen and Bill Arnot all keep their vintage aircraft in hangars at the airport. Nelson Ezell, who also runs a restoration business that has turned out some excellent restorations over the past few years, maintains many of the aircraft at the field.

Howard Pardue retired as a major in the United States Marine Corps, where he flew many different types of jet fighters. ("The F-8 Crusader was my favorite," he stated. "A great plane, beautifully responsive.") After leaving the Corps, he pretty much left flying behind and settled into the oil business—until he was introduced to general aviation as a way of getting around the vast area of Texas and purchased a Beech Bonanza as a private business plane.

One thing led to another, and Pardue found himself getting involved in the warbird movement just as the restoration and flying of vintage aircraft was beginning to mushroom. Pardue had never given much thought to the propeller-driven veterans of World War II, but once he began visiting a few warbird shows he became enthusiastic. The die was cast.

Pardue's distinct preference for the Navy and Marine fighters of World War II became obvious when he began buying fighters for what eventually became a large and significant private collection. He found a tubby Grumman Wildcat at Paris, Texas, that was in need of a new owner. The little Wildcat was the Navy's first successful monoplane retractable-gear fighter. This example had been marginally maintained in flying condition over the years but was desperately in need of a total restoration. Pardue made a deal for the Wildcat, and after a complete rebuild and new engine, a beautiful vintage fighter appeared that was an

continued on page 94

Here is a typical line-up at the annual Breckenridge Air Museum air show. What a fabulous array of Corsair fighters! Besides the Corsairs, the display is a virtual gallery of American World War II naval aviation, including Wildcats and Avengers.

46
46
46
MARINES

continued from page 92
immediate hit on the growing air show circuit.

The Wildcat was developed by Grumman (also known as the Iron Works) as a replacement for the biplane fighters of the day. It incorporated many innovations (at least for US Navy aircraft), including retractable landing gear (manually retracted by frantically turning a crank in the cockpit), enclosed cockpit and fairly heavy armament.

When America entered World War II, the Wildcat was in production and service. Although inferior in many ways to the Japanese Mitsubishi Zero, the Wildcat was a rugged and maneuverable aircraft that could exploit the enemy's weaknesses (lack of armor protection, non-sealing fuel tanks). During the dark early months of the war, United States Marine Corps and Navy Wildcats fought valiantly—either delaying the enemy (at the heroic stand on Wake Island) or meeting and destroying the Japanese in such godforsaken locations as Guadalcanal.

The Wildcat fought through the entire war, but, as with most early fighters, when the war was over the survivors were quickly scrapped. The fighters were too old for continued operation, the reserve forces had newer aircraft to choose from and the planes were too primitive to send to America's Third World allies. A few were purchased by civilian owners, who used them for a task Grumman had never dreamed of: spraying crops!

Pardue's Wildcat, built under license by the Eastern Division of General Motors, is a rare FM-2P variant (Navy Bureau Number 86777). The P stands for photographic; a couple camera ports and cameras were installed in the roomy fuselage, and the plane was used for armed reconnaissance.

Pardue quickly began gathering more round-engine warbirds, including a whole collection of Corsairs and a Grumman TBM-3 Avenger fondly known as the *Turkeycat.* Carrying civil registration N88HP (Navy Bureau Number 53522), the big Grumman, powered by a Wright R-2600 radial with 1900 hp, was a true hero of World War II: a rugged torpedo bomber with a three-man crew that could slug it out with the best the Japanese had to offer. (*Rugged* is a term often used for Grumman-built aircraft.) Well-armed, the Avenger played havoc with the fleet of the Imperial Japanese Navy.

One young Navy pilot named George Bush did his part against the enemy flying an Avenger in strikes against Japanese shipping. Bush was shot down in his Avenger during a Pacific battle, but he went on to other careers. A group of treasure hunters announced in late 1988 that they had discovered the wreckage of Bush's Avenger on the ocean floor.

After Pardue purchased his Avenger, he had it restored and painted in World War II configuration, thinking it would be an excellent addition to his collection of United States Navy and Marine aircraft. The Avenger is not flown frequently, but it is usually seen in the air during the annual Breckenridge Airshow.

Howard Pardue is directly responsible for almost doubling the number of surviving flyable Chance Vought Corsairs in the United States. The Corsair, known by various nicknames including Bent Wing Bird, Hose Nose and Whistling Death, was the most famous Marine Corps fighter of World War II. Fast, heavily armored and well armed, it wrought havoc on the Japanese Zeros.

After a difficult gestation period, during which the Corsair could not be

continued on page 96

Everything down and smoke on, Pardue displays the Bearcat in "dirty" configuration. Offering sterling performance, the Bearcat would have been heavily employed in the invasion of Japan—had not the atomic bomb brought a sudden and premature end to World War II.

14
14
14

continued from page 94
made carrier-compatible, the Marines were given the aircraft to operate off their primitive land bases in the island-hopping war leading toward Japan. It was an immediate success, and the Marines began to blast the Japs from the skies in prodigious quantities.

The Corsair will always be associated with Marine Corps aviation, especially through the exploits of Pappy Boyington and his Black Sheep Squadron. When the Corsair was made carrier-compatible Navy pilots immediately increased its fame, and the fighter also did well flying with the British Royal Navy.

During World War II, production of vital aircraft often taxed the parent company's facilities, and licenses were established with other builders so that the flow of combat aircraft to the front could increase. One of Pardue's Corsairs is a Goodyear-built FG-1D registered N67HP and painted in the markings of Marine fighter squadron VMF-111. Pardue had this aircraft equipped with a second seat directly behind the pilot's and a smoke system for a graceful aerobatic demonstration he had worked out with the Corsair.

In the sleepy Central American nation of Honduras, a couple dozen Chance Vought Corsairs of several different models constituted the country's main air defense from the late fifties through the early eighties. These former Navy fighters were based mainly at the air force headquarters near the town of Tegucigalpa and replaced a mixed

continued on page 98

They fought with what they had. In the dark early days of World War II, American pilots went into combat with the stubby Wildcat fighters—and did well against enemy aircraft that were superior not only in numbers but also in performance. Pardue is seen in the lead with his rare FM-2P; Jack Gaulding flies wing in the Confederate Air Force's FM-2. About a dozen Wildcats are still flying.

USS RANGER
VF-41
41-F-4
CONFEDERATE AIR FORCE
5

continued from page 96
bag of Lockheed Lightnings and Bell Kingcobras. The situation in the small nation was not all that peaceful, and the Corsairs were called upon several times to bomb and strafe rebels that threatened the government.

In 1969, at a major soccer game with neighboring Salvador, ethnic and political sentiments came to a boiling point, and the two nations went to war. Salvador was equipped with FG-1D Corsairs and P-51D Mustangs (most of which were brought south by American mercenary pilots), and several aerial combats ensued. Honduran Captain Fernando de Soto accounted for three Salvadoran aircraft (a mix of Mustangs and Corsairs). The war was short, fairly violent and marked the last time World War II propeller-driven fighters faced each other in open combat.

After the war, the Honduran fleet of Corsairs became increasingly less airworthy, and Howard Pardue and a partner were able to purchase the survivors, including a number of disassembled airframes and lots of spare parts. The mixture of F4U-4 and F4U-5N night fighters made a healthy injection into the American warbird community, although two have since been destroyed in accidents in the States.

Pardue kept several of the Corsairs for himself, selling the rest off to finance the cost of the expedition. An era in military aviation had come to a close, but a new era in warbird aviation had come alive.

Although Pardue sponsors the CAF's Merlin-powered Spitfire, his main interest in warbird aviation is
continued on page 100

Pardue found his Wildcat at a small airstrip in Paris, Texas, neglected and in need of lots of tender loving care. After purchasing the aircraft, he had it completely rebuilt, installing a new Wright R-1820 radial. It is now one of the most active of the surviving Wildcats.

5

continued from page 98

with the fighters powered by the massive Wright and Pratt & Whitney radial engines that offered Navy and Marine fighters plenty of horsepower and reliability—especially vital when operating over vast stretches of the Pacific. The American radial engines were never rivaled by those of the enemy, and they established a whole new generation of American aeronautical expertise.

A favorite aircraft in the Pardue stable is the ultrarare Grumman XF8F-1 Bearcat. The Bearcat is powered by the same engine as the Corsair: the Pratt & Whitney R-2800. Yet the Bearcat is a much smaller fighter than the Corsair and displays sparkling performance. Grumman engineers succeeded in creating a muscle plane that was at the same time graceful and overwhelmingly powerful.

Designed as a replacement for the Grumman Hellcat, the Bearcat offered better performance and maneuverability and was able to fly off small escort carriers. At this time, Japanese kamikaze pilots threatened America's Pacific fleet, and a hot, high-performance aircraft like the F8F was needed to get in the air quickly to intercept and destroy the incoming suicide attacks.

The first XF8F-1 was flown on 31 August 1944, and carried only four .50 caliber Browning air-cooled machine guns to help reduce weight. From its first flights, the Bearcat displayed exceptional performance, and contracts were soon awarded to produce the plane in the thousands. Squadron VF-19 was the first

continued on page 102

Pardue's Turkeycat, *registered NX88HP, is the famous Grumman TBM-3 Avenger, hero of many World War II Pacific battles. The Avenger was designed as a torpedo bomber and was a big, rugged aircraft that could take on the best the enemy could offer. Powered by a Wright R-2600 radial, it is surprisingly agile.*

continued from page 100
squadron to deploy the plane in May 1945. Although the atomic bomb put an end to production of the Bearcat, some limited production of the F8F-2, an improved variant, continued after the war.

Only 1,263 Bearcats were built, and few survived scrapping after they were withdrawn from service. The few that did survive became highly desirable during the sixties as air racers and ultimate single-engine fun machines. Today, the few Bearcats left (about a dozen) are much in demand and rarely come on the market.

Pardue's Bearcat, one of a small group of prototypes built for testing the new fighter, spent many years stored with the National Air and Space Museum. When Darryl Greenamyer traded his record-breaking F8F-2 Bearcat racer to the museum, he obtained the XF8F-1 in exchange. He then sold the fighter to George Enhorning, who brought the aircraft back to airworthiness after its many years of storage. Enhorning then sold the plane to Pardue, who installed a smoke system and immediately began hitting the air show circuit in the early eighties. With plenty of reserve power from the R-2800, the Bearcat makes an ideal air show machine. Pardue takes the rare fighter to the annual Reno Air Races, where it is gently put to its paces around the pylons.

Each year, in the last week of May, Pardue and the Breckenridge Air Museum invite warbirds from around the United States to participate in a week of Texas hospitality and fun flying. All this culminates in a public air show on Sunday that draws a large
continued on page 105

Howard Pardue prepares to start the FG-1D's R-2800 radial prior to another airshow performance.

HOWARD E PARDUE
MAJOR USMC
67

HP
MARINES
VMF 223
68

continued from page 102
crowds to see many vintage aircraft tearing up the sky.

Howard Pardue and this small Texas airport have definitely established themselves as one of the last bastions of the muscle plane.

F4U-4 NX68HP is flown here by Pardue. This is one of the aircraft that was operated by Honduras and saw action in the 1969 war with El Salvador. Armed with six .50 caliber machine guns, the -4 variant of the Corsair recorded many successes in World War II and Korea.

HP
MARINES
VMF III
FG-1D
MARINES
NX67HP

Previous page
The mountains in the background are a giveaway that this isn't Breckenridge—it's Chino, California, on a rare clear day. Pardue has the smoke system on in his Goodyear-built FG-1D Corsair, registered NX67HP, which is painted in the markings of Marine fighter squadron VMF-111.

Radial power unites as Howard Pardue in his Bearcat leads an eclectic formation comprising the CAF's FM-2 Wildcat and J. K. Ridley's F4U-4 Corsair, registered N4908M—another of the Corsairs that Pardue returned from the Honduran Air Force.

Pardue maintains his XF8F-1 in perfect condition, as this photograph illustrates.

US Navy's big stick: Carrier Attack Wing

Few American weapon systems are more expensive than the aircraft carrier . . . and few are more effective. America's attack carrier force is unique in world military might; even the Soviets' growing carrier force does not approach the United States' fleet in numbers or firepower.

Constantly a point of heated debate between Democrats and Republicans, the tremendous cost and time involved in building, fitting out and making operational a new carrier are often issues that involve several presidential administrations. During the seventies, Admiral Elmo Zumwalt proposed a change in US Navy concepts that would see a larger number of smaller carriers, which would increase America's seagoing power while offering a more budget-minded system to politicians. After gaining considerable favor this plan was abandoned, and the only carriers constructed today are gigantic 90,000 ton monsters that extend American influence to remote parts of the world like the Persian Gulf. The latest of these to become operational was the USS *Theodore Roosevelt*, CVN-71 (the *N* stands for nuclear; all such ships are now nuclear powered).

Current military planning sees the commissioning of one attack carrier every three to four years as part of a plan to build up US Navy

continued on page 113

The sun rising over the Atlantic silhouettes a Tomcat from VF-101, which had been securely chained down the previous night. The rough weather conditions at sea mean that every attempt must be made to carefully secure aircraft to the flight and hangar decks.

134
506

continued from page 110
ship numbers to the magic 600 figure. However, in February 1988, Defense Secretary Carlucci's budget cuts caused that ambitious plan to be scaled back and saw the resignation of Secretary of the Navy (and popular novelist) James Webb in protest.

The US Navy has a long history of successful carrier operations in World War II and Korea, and now has two Sixth Fleet carriers keeping a watchful eye in the waters surrounding the Middle East. Its long-term plan is to field fifteen carriers as the main components of fifteen carrier battle groups. To complete this plan, two more *Nimitz*-class carriers are heading toward operational status. The Navy sees this number of carriers as essential for protecting American seagoing interests while being able to respond quickly to almost any trouble spot in the world.

Planners estimate that current *Nimitz* carriers have a life span of fifty years—a length of time that helps dilute criticism of high cost. America's allies are "carrier poor." The French are capable of fielding two 30,000 ton carriers (to be eventually replaced by smaller nuclear carriers), while Britain, Spain and India operate smaller 20,000 ton vessels that accommodate British Aerospace Sea Harrier VTOL fighter/attack aircraft.
continued on page 116

The morning sun highlights the weathered and patched low-visibility paint of a VF-101 Tomcat. VF-101 is the East Coast Tomcat RAG and is based at NAS Oceana, Virginia.

Next page
Tail hook down, a Grim Reapers F-14A prepares to catch a cable. The Tomcat constitutes the Carrier Air Group's main line of aerial defense, able to meet and defeat a variety of airborne enemy threats a great distance from where the battle group is steaming.

173

AD
NAVY

continued from page 113

Newport News Shipbuilding began constructing the USS *Theodore Roosevelt* in September 1980 as the fourth member of the *Nimitz* class (earlier ships were the *Nimitz,* the *Dwight D. Eisenhower* and the *Carl Vinson*).

The *Roosevelt* established new ground for itself by using a modular construction technique that saw individual modules of up to 900 tons being built and prefitted with needed internal equipment, machinery, piping and electrical units. These modules were then lifted by crane and assembled into the overall ship. This method was a success and was responsible for the *Roosevelt* being delivered some seventeen months ahead of schedule.

The carrier was launched from the shipyard on 27 October 1984, and fitting out for initial sea trials began. A commanding officer for the ship was named in February 1984, but it was not until May 1986 that the crew began moving aboard. Sea trials started in September 1986, and the carrier was commissioned on 25 October 1986. This time schedule gives some idea of the complex task of preparing a supercarrier for operational duty.

With its home port at Norfolk, Virginia, the *Roosevelt* was assigned to the Atlantic fleet. Heavy workup duties leading to operational status began late in 1987, and CVN-71 was assigned its own air wing, CVW-8.

A typical carrier air wing has between eighty and ninety aircraft. Two squadrons of Grumman F-14A Tomcats are usually included for

continued on page 118

This VF-101 Tomcat undergoes engine runs after being secured in its parking space. The squadron leader ranks painted on the canopy frame indicate that both officers aboard the plane were on temporary detached duty from the RAF *to the US Navy.*

SQD LDR SIMON BRYANT
SQD LDR JOHN McGARRY
134
VF101

continued from page 116
defense duties, along with two squadrons of A-7 Corsair IIs for light attack, one squadron of Grumman A-6E Intruders for all-weather attack, a "minisquadron" of four electronic-countermeasures Grumman EA-6B Prowlers and a squadron of Grumman E-2C Hawkeyes for Airborne Electronic Warfare duties. Two Anti-Submarine Warfare squadrons are also carried, one with Lockheed S-3A Vikings and one with SH-3H helicopters. With the replacement of A-7s by McDonnell Douglas FA-18 Hornets, however, the composition of air wings is changing.

Air wing CVW-8 is equipped with two F/A-18 squadrons, VFA-15 and VFA-87, which both have their home port at NAS Cecil Field in Florida. Air wing CVW-8 is also accommodating a change undertaken by air wing CVW-3 aboard the USS *John F. Kennedy*. This change is the embarking of a second medium attack squadron, VA-36 joining VA-35. These two units fly the efficient TRAM (Target Recognition and Attack Multisensor) equipped A-6E. VA-35, the Black Panthers, is the Navy's oldest attack squadron.

Since the retirement of the RF-8 Crusader, the US Navy does not have a dedicated reconnaissance aircraft, and this duty is taken up by F-14As equipped with a TARPS pod that allows the plane to take high-quality photographs of specific targets. A proposed RF/A-18 Hornet is still in the planning stage.

When all aircraft are deployed, even the *Roosevelt's* 1,100 foot long deck and large hangar bays become crowded. The operation of ninety aircraft from such a deck is complex and dangerous, requiring a dedicated and skilled crew to make everything happen as planned.

The carrier is as self-sufficient as it can be, but when possible vital items are flown on board by COD (carrier onboard delivery) aircraft. CVN-71 has its own engine workshop located in a small area below decks at its stern. The shop is responsible for the repair and operation of all nine types of engines used by the aircraft operating from the ship.

Knowing the ship's military value, the Soviets have placed considerable resources toward destroying it. Unlike World War II carriers, however, the *Roosevelt* has somewhat limited defense armament. The carrier relies on outlying ships and its own aircraft to provide an effective defensive umbrella. Outer perimeter defense is taken up by F-14A Tomcats with their Phoenix missile system. The Tomcats provide CAP (Combat Air Patrol) for the entire battle group and are tasked with destroying intruding enemy aircraft, particularly the new generation of Soviet cruise missile launchers. Guided missile cruisers provide another line of defense for the carrier. The next layer of defense is provided by Sea Sparrow surface-to-air missiles, and close-in attacks are handled by the awesome power of the Phalanx radar-aimed rotary cannon. Once a missile or aircraft has penetrated this far, the carrier will probably receive some form of damage even though the enemy aircraft or missile is successfully destroyed.

During my visit aboard the *Roosevelt* in early 1988, the carrier was operating off Jacksonville, Florida, doing carquals (carrier qualifications) with a number of East Coast RAG (Replacement Air Group) training squadrons. The major units of CVW-8 had yet to embark, but the SH-3H helicopters of HS-9, the "Sea Griffins," were already installed onboard, having been tasked with providing helicopter support for the carqual period.

Since the air wing was not aboard, the carrier was comparatively empty with "only" 3,300 men and 150 officers. The total number rises to about 6,300 when the air wing is aboard.

The massive deck was alive with activity as F-14As from VF-101 ("Grim Reapers"), A-6Es from VA-42 ("Green Pawns") and E-2Cs from VAW-120 came and went with rapid regularity. The action was intense because there was only a limited amount of time for crews to get their needed launches and traps, and operations went on well into the night.

A night launch of a Tomcat with afterburners blazing is a scene right out of Dante—afterburner launches are usually reserved for pilots just becoming familiar with the type because the Tomcat, combined with the carrier's powerful catapults, can easily become airborne without the fuel-guzzling burners.

March 1988 saw CVW-8 embarking aboard the *Roosevelt* at Norfolk. With that move, the 97,000 ton nuclear-powered carrier, with 6,300 personnel and representing a multibillion dollar investment, became a vital part of America's defensive posture and a strong warning to possible enemies about treading upon ground where they should not.

Perched high in his near-bubble canopy, a VA-42 pilot observes the actions of the deck crew as they ready the Intruder for launch.

535
RESCUE
HAND GRIP
JET
INTAKE
DANGER

This VA-42 A-6E is just about ready to get the signal to launch while a Grumman E-2C Hawkeye executes a go-around in the background.

532

535

Everyone's a critic. The deck crew watches as a VA-42 Intruder approaches the Roosevelt*'s flight deck for a touch-and-go. VA-42 is East Coast RAG A-6.*

FLY I

The Hawkeye is a large aircraft, and it must be carefully directed while on the flight deck—those big propellers could do lots of harm to an unaware deck crew member.

Looking like he's carrying a heavy load of extra-large chain mail, this deck crewman is responsible for securely lashing the aircraft to their parking spots.

It gets hot in there! Completely covered by his protective suit, a Roosevelt *fireman stands by during flight operations.*

With the catapult still steaming from its previous launch, the pilot of a Tomcat is positioned for his turn at launch. This late-evening view shows that even the dull, flat camouflage now worn by most Naval combat aircraft is still capable of reflecting a modicum of light.